Full Paranoid Mode

By Tim T. Neymor

Take that as you will. It is the only way for this information to be made available to the public.

Copyright

Dedication

I want to dedicate this book to the one person who made this possible. Without her, I would not be here. Without her, I would never have been able to write this or any book ever. She took my inability to write more than one paragraph, and turned it into the ability to write an entire book. She turned my hatred of writing into a thing of joy. She is truly amazing.

To Amazing A.
Thank you for this book.
Thank you for my life.

Prologue

Full Paranoid Mode is the extreme case of paranoia where you believe everyone is out to get you. Full Paranoid Mode is also a mode you can use to start looking at things in a way you have not seen before.

Use this state of mind sparingly, to be aware of what's really going on. If you want to do something about the things you learn here, good luck. This is not a manual of what to do: it is information on what is happening. What you do with this information is up to you. But really, is your life so bad that you want to change it? Have The Powers That Be made a good life or a bad life for you? Do you really want to mess that up? Do you really want to upset "them"?

Table of Contents

Chapter 1
Light And Sound

Light bulbs let you see in the dark. But they also let certain government agencies hear you talk.

Back in the 1800s light bulbs were designed around the same time as phonograph recordings, and by the same person: Thomas Edison. That was no coincidence.

One of Edison's early designs for recording voices involved a glass bulb. Glass vibrates well in response to human voices. If you have ever seen commercials or demonstrations showing a wine glass vibrating and shattering in response to a person singing a high note, you will know how well glass picks up human vocal sounds. Another example of how well glass and the human voice interact was publicized in the 1980s. It was discovered that some countries were using lasers pointed at windows in foreign embassies to pick up and read vibrations the voices inside those rooms were making on the window glass. Measuring slight variations in vibrations from laser light allowed them to figure out what was being said in those rooms. Glass responds very well to sound vibrations.

Edison's glass bulbs picked up sound vibrations and transmitted them through a series of wide metal grooves that caught the sound range of human voices, converting them into electrical signals. Those big threads at the base of light bulbs are wide to optimally pick up sound waves of human voices. Consider that all electrical connections, including all other lights designed when Edison's light bulb was invented, were very small in comparison. There was no other valid reason for those wide grooves.

While this design worked well for general sound recording, it was considered too fragile, often breaking when people would handle it while trying to talk into it.

1

But there was a side effect of this design: part of the wire that would help capture and carry some of the sound glowed rather brightly. This became the basis of the light bulb.

There were several light bulb designs back then, but only one optimally picked up sound because it was specifically designed to do that. Edison's microphone was that light bulb. Edison's design was promoted over all others to the point that people believed he invented the first electric light. He didn't. But to this day people still believe it, and still use Edison's light.

The Powers That Be realized people could be fooled into putting these "light bulbs" into their places of business and houses to light up rooms. This allowed agencies to hear everything that went on in those rooms. But there needed to be a way to get sounds from those rooms back to the secret centers to record and store them. That is when they came up with the idea of running electric lines to everyone's businesses and homes. If people thought they were getting electricity to run those light bulbs, they would welcome those lines with open arms. It worked. No one complained about those massive electric lines running into every home and business in the country. No one noticed that there was more than one line running into their homes.

There is one line for running an electric current into your home. But there is more than one line running into your home. Why?

There have been various explanations for the extra lines. For example, a "return phase". If the electricity is being returned, why are you charged for it and why does it need to be produced again? Or a ground wire. But all buildings have a ground wire that actually goes into the structure or ground, not back to the electric company.

These and other cover stories are continually given to distract you from the truth: that extra line is taking electric impulses from light bulbs derived from the sounds in every room, and is transmitting them back to a central facility where the information is kept to do whatever they want with it.

While they were successful in getting people to install light bulbs in every room of every building, and successful in installing electric lines to transmit your conversations back to them, they still did not get everybody.

The biggest groups that were unreachable were self-sustaining types: survivalists, hippy-environmentalists and extremist groups. While all of those people used light bulbs, they tended to be off-grid, meaning they produced their own electricity and did not let electric lines run into their buildings. Because those groups generated their own electricity, they were interested in using as little electricity as possible to light their buildings. So The Powers That Be came up with a light bulb that used far less electricity, and at the same time transmitted all collected sounds wirelessly to nearby receivers. This is the fluorescent light bulb.

All fluorescent bulbs have a ballast, which changes electric current into a form that the gasses in the bulb need to light correctly. But the real reason for these ballasts is to change collected voice data into a radio signal and transmit it to hidden receivers. If you look on the ballasts themselves, or on the packaging fluorescent bulbs come in, they blatantly state that the ballasts transmit a radio signal. And in the style of humor The Powers That Be seem to enjoy, they state part of what they are doing in the name of the object itself. "Ballast" means an object that weighs you down in order to increase control, as in keeping you under their control.

As The Powers That Be increased their monitoring of everyone in buildings, they also wanted their spying power to continue when people were outside. Outdoor lighting was promoted as a safety device: safer for them to hear more of what you are saying. Street lamps that were low to the ground were implemented everywhere. As technology increased the ability of light bulbs to hear you from farther away, street lights were put up higher for greater coverage of listening area. The same technology that increased light bulb's listening range also changed the color of the light output. That is why all those large street lights now put out a yellow-orange color instead of the old standard white color.

Over the years advances in technology have shrunk the size of many electrical devices. This also includes light bulbs that pick up your conversations. The technology has gotten so small that what you say can be picked up with just a tiny dot of a light. Those dots of lights, often red or green or blue, have been put on every device imaginable: from coffee pots to watches to TVs to car alarm systems and so much more. If you turn off all the lights in a modern household, there remain numerous small lights everywhere, all picking up the conversations you have in the dark.

If you notice the size of microphones you see in old TV shows and movies, they were about the size of light bulbs. And today, you can see on a cell phone the tiny hole that picks up your voice is about the size of a tiny LED light. Light bulbs have shrunk in size in step with microphones shrinking in size. This is no coincidence. These two items are based on the same technology.

Where can you have a conversation without anyone listening to you?

You would think going outside would be safe. But if you have a flashlight with you, they can listen through that light bulb too. You didn't think it really took two "C" or "D" size batteries to run that tiny light bulb did you? The reason flashlight batteries go dead so soon is because they use a lot of juice to boost the radio signal to be transmitted over long distances, like when you are out hiking in the woods away from everyone (except them). And just how do they transmit a radio signal?

That spring in the base of flashlights holding the batteries in place is actually a wound up antenna wire. Some flashlights that use a flat piece of metal instead of a wound spring are actually using the more advanced flat metal antennas like those found in cell phones. Both antenna types send your conversations in the form of radio waves to listening stations.

If you stand outside you can be seen by satellites and they can use you location to alert listening stations in the area to pick up your conversation.

The only place to have a safe conversation is under a tree. Specifically, a pine tree. Pine needles and pine sap are the only things that prevents all satellite and ground listening stations from picking up your conversations. Pine needles and sap interfere with sight, sound, and radio signals.

Government agencies knew about this interference from pine trees long ago, which is why they promoted a tradition from a small sect of one religion, making it into a main holiday tradition for everyone to perform. People are encouraged to go out and cut pine trees down, take them home, wrap them up in light bulbs, lots of light bulbs, and put presents under those trees. This is to stop you from getting under the tree. But even if you do, those numerous light bulbs will overcome the pine needle interference and transmit your conversation back to them.

Chapter 2
Cash Serial Number Tracking

People are trained to think that if you avoid electronic payments and pay in cash, you can avoid anyone tracking your purchases. But if you look at the paper money in your wallet, every bill has its own serial number. That combined with the year and other numbers on the bill make for a unique numerical fingerprint for each and every single paper dollar in every denomination out there. The public reason for this is supposedly to stop people from counterfeiting those dollars. But this system has never stopped anyone from trying to counterfeit money.

Note that dollar coins do not have any serial numbers on them. The government's half-hearted attempt at distributing dollar coins has met with failure every time. This is not due to the public's distaste for coins. It is because the government sabotages these attempts through the use of several psychological and mechanical distribution means. They do not want those coins to succeed.

What they really want is for the unique serial number bills to be the main form of cash used so they can track every single monetary transaction.

When you get cash from an ATM, it records the serial numbers of those bills and sends that information to the government. When spending that money at any modern store, either you slide it into a slot in a self-serve machine which reads those serial numbers and identifies your purchases, or you hand it to a cashier who seems to just lay it in a section in a drawer. What you don't see are the security cameras recording not only you but also the serial numbers on those bills. Do you ever notice how cashiers always move the bills from one hand to the other as if they are just counting the money? They are actually making sure the full front of each bill is visible to those security cameras. Cashiers do not know the reason they are doing this. They are simply trained to do this with all paper bills.

You also get a receipt for your purchase. If you use a credit card, the entire purchase is tied to you in electronic records. But this also happens with cash purchases. The ATM you get money from connects those specific bills to you. When spending them at a store, those bills are identified as coming from you and they are recorded in those same electronic purchase records, just as if you had used a credit card with your name on it. The receipt will say cash, but it has your name in a hidden part of that electronic record.

Even if you simply hand cash to someone else to spend, when that person spends it, tracking programs now know you are associated with that person. This becomes very important when you realize that all illegal transactions are normally done with cash. You withdraw ten cash bills from an ATM. Suppose that a known drug dealer deposits those same ten bills in his own account two days later. The government now knows you buy drugs from that dealer. This process works in cases of drugs, gambling, prostitution, bribes, and all sorts of illegal activity. It builds a profile of who you interact with, in order to increase their knowledge of your entire life.

While serial number tracking has been in use for decades, radio signal tracking has now become more feasible. Those new security strips in bills are radio ID tags, allowing the trackers to scan your unique cash bills from far away. How far? Satellite far. You have heard that satellites from their orbits high in space can see well enough to read the words on a book you are holding. But it is not just the visible wavelengths of the electromagnetic spectrum that they can detect. It is all wavelengths of the electromagnetic spectrum that they can detect. That includes radio wavelengths which can detect those security strips in new cash bills in your wallet that you just got from the ATM.

They don't need to wait for you to make a purchase anymore. They know what you are doing with your cash even when you are doing nothing with it at all.

Chapter 3
Cell Phone Batteries

There are lots of ways to tap into cell phones. Depending on the way someone accesses your cell phone, they could download your pictures, record your calls, listen to you after you hang up, track your position to find you, or even make calls from your phone without you knowing it. The safest thing to do to prevent access to your phone when you are not talking on it is to remove the battery. You won't get any calls or texts, but no one will be able to locate or listen to you. This is especially useful if you want to go somewhere without being tracked, or to have a private in-person conversation without anyone else eavesdropping. This procedure of removing the battery is shown on TV shows and movies as the way to stop all that tracking of you.

But if they are showing it to you on TV, that is because they want you to believe it in order for them to spy on you.

How can they still track and listen to you even when you have the battery out of your phone? Simply by activating the hidden battery in your phone.

A battery is pretty much two different metals pressed against each other that allow for different electrical charges in them to create an electric current. All it takes is two specific types of metal to make a battery.

If you look at modern round cell batteries used for hearing aids and other small devices, you can see how small batteries can get. If you would unroll that battery metal out flat, you would come up with a very thin battery about half the size of a small cell phone. That is exactly what happened.

Some of the material in your cell phone body is really the metals for a battery. When you remove the regular battery from your phone, you activate this hidden battery. It is not very powerful, but it is enough to broadcast any conversation you are having and transmit your location.

The two activities of listening to you and tracking your location are always running on your cell phone, no matter what apps you turn off or even if you turn your phone completely off. Those spy programs are built into the hardware of every cell phone. Nothing on your phone can detect them.

Spy programs use your phone's regular battery first. This is why it drains so quickly, even when you have all other apps turned off and your phone itself is turned off. Batteries in other devices that are turned off normally last for months. But in cell phones that are turned off they last for days, not months, due to the spy programs always running.

The hidden battery activates only when your primary battery has been removed or is completely drained. When the primary battery is drained, the owner of that phone puts it on a charger right away. Both the primary and hidden batteries recharge when you charge your cell phone. This is why recharging takes so long. You are actually recharging two batteries.

The hidden battery is therefore used for only short periods of time and does not need all that much power to accomplish its job.

The hidden battery cannot be accessed for any of the cell phone's regular functions. It is directly connected to the hardware based spy programs and is used as a backup when other power sources (battery, wall plug, charging stand) fail.

With the addition of cameras to cell phones and smart phones and tablets, hardware based spy programs were updated to also use the camera to spy on you. Transmitting images takes more power than transmitting sound and location data. The first camera phones had low resolution pictures due to the hidden battery's power limit to transmit images, not due to technical limits of putting a camera on a cell phone. As the technology of hidden batteries has increased in power, so has the resolution of cell phone cameras. But to save hidden battery power and transmit longer, spy programs on your phone still send lower resolution images than your cell phone camera is capable of. They only need to see who is doing what in view of your phone. They don't care how pretty it looks.

The low resolution images along with sound and location data give them all they need to determine pretty much everything you do when you are near your cell phone. The next time you want to have a private conversation in a hidden location with no one watching you, leave your cell phone at home.

Chapter 4
Humans Not From Earth

Ever wonder why we humans, who supposedly evolved on this planet, breath oxygen when the atmosphere on earth consists of only 20% oxygen but 78% nitrogen? It's because humans did not originate on this planet. We are transplants from a planet where the atmosphere is almost all (at least 80%) oxygen. This planet's low oxygen atmosphere keeps our brains from working at full capacity, which explains a lot of human stupidity. We are being dumbed down to be taken advantage of by those who put us here.

Another mismatch to this planet is our sleep cycle. This planet has a 24 hour day. The farther back in time you go, the shorter this planet's day was. It started out spinning at a faster rate than it is now. It has slowed down over the past few billion years. So you would think that our wake-sleep cycle would either match the current day-night cycle or be a shorter cycle evolved from an earlier time. But the truth is that not only does our independent wake-sleep cycle not match the current 24 hour day, it is longer than that, not shorter.

There have been repeated sleep tests that remove all references to time (clocks, watches, etc) and remove all view of sunlight by putting people deep underground, or in completely enclosed rooms. These studies last for weeks to let people's own independent wake-sleep cycle show through by having them wake and sleep whenever they want. All these studies show the same thing. Human being's natural independent wake-sleep cycle is much longer than 24 hours. In fact it is closer to about 30 hours. That is a rather large difference. Something too large to be accounted for by any known variable. The planet we came from had a longer day. Our internal wake-sleep cycle is still tuned to that planet. This is why people have a tendency to want to stay up late all the time, and want to sleep in all the time too. We are continually trying to follow our original day-night cycle.

The reduction of our natural amount of sleep every day has resulted in our continuously being tired and not able to think clearly, which has the effect of also dumbing us down. This is intentional by those who brought us here.

The evidence of being from another planet does not stop there. Think of what you eat. Have you ever truly had a hunger craving for an unaltered plant or animal from this planet? Or have you instead had cravings for foods that are only altered products? Chocolate, ice cream, alcohol, steak (one small super-heated cut part from an animal that has been altered by strict diet and hormones, and a flavor added like salt or pepper or steak sauce). These and other items that most people will crave at some point in their life are not naturally from here. They may not be natural from anywhere. But our craving for them is a rejection of the natural foods of this planet. It is our body's way of saying "not the plants and animals from here, anything but the plants and animals from here." We don't have the option of our own planet's plants and animals, so we seek artificial substitutions.

Not only is the food from this planet off from our body design, the water is off too.

Our body is mostly water, and we are told that our internal water salt content matches the salt content of the oceans. Yet if you try to drink ocean water, you will die of too much salt in your system. That is not a match. And the only other water on earth is fresh water: lakes, streams, rain. You can drink that water, but if you stay in it too long, your skin gets wrinkled and can eventually deteriorate, just as if you were in an acid bath. That does not match your internal water either. There is no water on this planet that truly matches the water inside us. This is because our internal water did not come from this planet, and neither did we.

The first people who arrived here from that other planet carried original water in their bodies. That internal water has been passed down from mother to child in every subsequent generation. And as each child grows, their body tries to assemble the correct molecules from what they eat and drink to form that same water balance inside their bodies every day. But where in the body is that original water kept? Where is the pure unadulterated sample that our bodies use to compare against every molecule we eat and drink to find the right ones to pull aside to replenish our form of water? What organ in our body is near the food and liquid we take in every day, and appears to have no known function? Our appendix.

Our appendix sits along the intestines, just alongside the path all food and liquid takes as it goes through our digestive system. It sits there sampling molecules of food and liquid to look for matches to its reservoir of our home planet's water. It grabs any molecule that matches anything in the reservoir to replenish the original supply of our water to keep our bodies going. But sometimes the foreign material from this planet overwhelms the original sample of home water. That foreign material then multiplies out of control expanding the appendix, rupturing it. Doctors will sometimes remove the appendix, leaving the person without a reservoir of original water. Such people may become more acclimated to the water here. But they never completely lose their connection to the home planet. There are other organs and systems in the human body that continuously try to keep us in line with our planet's natural systems. Though they are not as effective as the appendix.

If you find yourself feeling tired, dull, and craving artificial foods, know that it is not you, it is this planet.

Chapter 5
Fracking Water

Fracking is the process of drilling deep into the earth and setting off explosives to fracture (or "frack") underground rock formations in order to release natural gas trapped in there. Drilling platforms drill bore holes for the explosives, then pump liquids (various unknown liquids including industrial waste) into the ground at high pressure to force the released natural gas up into collection sites.

This process is supposed to not disturb ground water supplies sitting above the fractured rock bed. But numerous examples have proven that fracking does in fact pollute these water supplies, sometimes beyond the point of usability. Various pollutants from the fractured rocks and from the liquids pumped into the ground end up in the ground water, making it completely unusable for human consumption. This has been treated as a small side accident by fracking companies. But the truth is, this is not an accident. It is the purpose of fracking.

Major international companies have been figuring out how to gain control of the earth's drinking water supply in order to charge every person on earth for its use. While they have figured out how to charge people in cities, they have not figured out how to charge people out in the country, people who just dig a well down anywhere from ten to a hundred feet and get fresh clean drinking water for free. Not only would these people not buy water from major international companies, they would actually be able to sell their own well water to others if water prices began climbing like the international companies want.

Those companies got the break they were looking for when a research firm published a paper on their problems trying to get natural gas from rocks deep within the earth. The problem was that some of the gas, along with some of the liquids they were using to pressure the gas upwards, was making its way up past presumably impermeable layers of rock and into water tables above the fractured rocks.

The idea of an impermeable layer of rock at certain levels in large areas of the U.S. is a geologic term that turns out to not be an accurate description. While these layers of rock do generally keep water from running down further into the earth, they are not an actual continuous single rock. This layer has been broken and fractured by very old earthquakes that occurred over millions of years while this layer formed and hardened. These cracked pieces had nowhere to go when broken by earthquakes and settled back together forming a good enough seal to prevent water above from running through the cracks. Even rocks that were pushed past each other in earthquakes settled together with the new rocks they were pushed up against. Think of what happens when you form a cup with your two hands. You can hold water in your two hands as long as they are pushed against each other. But if you take them apart, all the water rushes out in the space between them. Your hands are separate from each other, and can be penetrated with enough pressure. This is what those impermeable layers of rock are like, and this is what happens when lower rock layers are shattered and liquid is pumped in below at high pressure.

The firm researching this method of natural gas extraction published information regarding water pollution it caused. International companies bent on world water control saw a solution to their own dilemma. The pollution was not a problem, it was a solution.

Areas that were ripe for natural gas extraction were also full of ground water supplies people were using for free. By using fracking to get natural gas, they could also pollute the ground water supplies and stop those "freeloaders" from disrupting their world water control plans.

But people living near these water supplies would not just let fracking companies pollute their water. So the international control companies simply lied about the pollution problem. And they gladly paid local people a lot of money from these fracking operations to stop any objections.

The thing about these payouts to locals is that they do not make economic sense from the amount of natural gas extracted and the costs of running a fracking operation. Looking at oil companies as an example, locals are usually pushed out of all money except for a rare few direct property owners. And oil sells for far more than natural gas. So why pay locals as much as they do? Because the economics are not based on the natural gas being extracted. The economics are based on destroying ground water supplies to prevent any future competition to the international water companies. When everyone has to pay a few companies for all usable water, that is when the huge profits will kick in. Getting some natural gas from these ground water destruction wells is just a minor side benefit.

These fracking operations are being set up everywhere on the planet that there is any ground water of any volume. At the rate of this fracking rush, it will be about another decade before all ground water is polluted beyond all possible use. Then the profits will start rolling in to the international water companies.

Fracking Networked Wires

Where would you go to avoid all satellite and listening devices that the government could use to track you? Underground, of course. As deep into the basement floors of a building as possible. And that is where they want you to go.

When you are standing on the bottom floor in the basement of a building, having a secret conversation, you are standing on top of a network of wires which are listening to everything you say. Ever notice how basements of buildings tend to not have carpet on the floor? That is so your voice does not get muffled when they listen to you through those floors.

Getting underneath a building to lay out a network of listening devices has been somewhat difficult, until fracking started.

Fracking operations drill a hole deep into the earth straight down, then sideways for miles. Explosives are then detonated in those side runs. And all rock that was nice and solid and protecting your basement from any external underground intruders is now all nice and fractured, easy to slide long runs of wire to directly under your basement.

Fracking operations are happening in remote rural areas. Buildings in these areas had been difficult to run underground wires to. Drilling operations that were needed to achieve wire placement were sometimes rather obvious. But with the advent of fracking, no one thinks anything about large drilling operations going on in all these remote areas. The rather blunt and blatant way of cracking rocks under buildings to run wires through is not an issue. No one cares about all the activity underground in their area when a fracking well is nearby.

Fracking People Pods

There are people in suspended animation in pods deep in the earth. They are waiting in deep sleep until anywhere from hundreds to millions of years in the future before being revived. They paid a company to put them there, hoping to come out into either a near future that will be a better place to live or a far future in which they won't have to contend with humans anymore. The company sets the pods several miles underground where they use earth's heat as a power source to keep the pods going until the specified wake up time. People are paying millions of dollars to do this.

Although the locations are secret, the way they are able to put pods down that deep are to use specialized drilling platforms disguised as natural gas fracking wells. They take advantage of the fact that the central U.S. has a long term stable geology. Very little chance of earthquake fractures crushing the pods, even over a million year time period. With all the fracking wells that are out there, no one is going to notice a few extra ones here and there, hiding in plain sight.

There were previous operations putting pods deep into the earth. But those operations mainly relied on abandoned mines: places that were known where people could gain access to if motivated enough. Extremely rich people who were paying for the chance to be in a suspended animation pod did not like the idea of the general public being able to find out where they were being buried. Companies offering deep earth suspended animation saw the increase of fracking in geologically stable areas and used that as a cover to set up their own platforms. They drill much deeper than fracking wells and set their rich clientele deep in the earth, in plain sight, unnoticed by people who can see "fracking" operations from their front porch.

If you happen to see a fracking drilling operation, look closely at what they are doing there. You might notice a weird looking pod going into the ground if you look close enough.

Chapter 6
Computer Upload Data

Computer operating systems like Windows, Apple and Linux copy all of your data (personal and work files, all your internet activity, chats, instant messages, everything you do) and hide it in empty areas of the operating system's (OS) files.

OS files run the basic computer. They activate when you start your computer, providing a framework for all the programs you use: like a web browser, spreadsheet or text program.

A computer file size is measured from the first byte to the last byte, no matter what is in between. Zeros and ones both count equally. Let's say you have the following two files:

10001

and

10111

They are both the same file size.

Operating system files are encoded so that no one can see what is in them. The first ten to thirty percent is useful information for the computer to use, then the rest is all zeros except for the last few bytes to end the file. OS's use this empty space to hide your data.

When your computer updates, it uploads OS files with your data to secret government computers. Then it downloads new OS files to your computer with empty space available again. This is why computers update so often; so agencies can continuously retrieve your data. They even clue you in to what they are doing. Update: as in "up" loading your "data".

This happens on cell phones too. Updates are less obvious, but they happen all the time. The question is why doesn't the government just send a copy of your files to their computers without hiding it in the OS files?

When computers first started to be used by regular people at home, internet connection was slow and sent over phone lines. But voice and internet could not be used simultaneously. If you were using the phone line for the internet, you could not make or receive a voice call. Any computer internet use was obvious because it blocked voice calls on the phone. Any unnecessary uploads would be obvious too by all the extra time it took for a set of your files to upload. So they hid your data inside operating system files and waited for OS update times, when people would normally leave their computer hooked up to the internet for a long period of time and walk away to do something else while the update finished. The fact that these OS updates would take an enormously long time did not bother anyone because everyone just assumed that it must take a long time for all those really big OS files to download. This setup worked well and has been in use ever since.

Internet speeds have been increasing so much that a copy of your data files could be made and uploaded at any time without you noticing the tiny amount of time it takes. However, some people are still on dial-up connections and therefore that same older system to hide uploaded data files is still needed. Even if a separate upload system that depended on your connection type and speed was used, laptops that are carried between connection types might accidentally use the wrong upload system, resulting in that extra upload being discovered. So everyone was left on that same old upload system just to make things easy.

You may think that you can hide your data files on your computer. But you have to remember that they built the operating system that pretty much *is* your computer. Everything that happens on a computer goes through the operating system. Nothing escapes detection. It would be like trying to hide a large box on someone's bed. It would be noticed no matter where you put it. And if you copy or move files to another computer or external disk drive or backup website, the process of copying and moving files requires the operating system to make that process happen. Those processes copy that data into those operating system file spaces too.

Your computer, cell phone, and smart phone all update their files every so often, and a copy of everything you have done on those devices - calls, text messages, websites visited, emails, etc. - is being sent to government computers without you ever noticing it. When those updates are done, you will have a fresh clean set of operating system files, waiting for you to start using your devices again.

Chapter 7
Gas Tanks Ten Percent

Oil companies have found a way to make you pay more for gas by giving you less. Newer car gas tanks have ten percent less capacity than stated to match gas pumps giving out ten percent less gas than stated on the pump. And your gas gauge on the dashboard is rigged to cover up that shortage. For example, if you are empty on a twenty gallon capacity gas tank and fill it up at a gas station, the gas pump will read twenty gallons and your gas gauge will read full. But only eighteen gallons will have gone into your actual eighteen gallon capacity gas tank, even though you are paying for twenty gallons.

If you calculate your mileage, you still will not know about the reduced capacity gas tank. You will be calculating mileage based on the number of gallons reported on the gas pump, which is the inflated number. If the gas pump shows twenty gallons added to your car, and you drove four hundred miles, you will think that you got twenty miles per gallon. But actually only eighteen gallons were added for that four hundred mile trip, which puts you closer to twenty two miles per gallon. Better mileage, but you won't know it. This is why fuel efficiency in new cars seems to have stalled out over the last decade. It really has improved, but the greed of oil companies has prevented you from getting the economic advantage of the better mileage.

There are still cars on the road with older full capacity gas tanks. They get the full amount of gas from gas pumps. How does a gas pump know when to dispense and display the full amount of gas or ten percent less? By identifying your car using those security cameras you see everywhere at gas stations. Those cameras that are supposedly for security were actually put there to identify newer cars with reduced capacity gas tanks. They send your car's image to a database that identifies if your car is the older full tank or newer ten percent reduced tank, then flip the pump display to match the car gas tank type. Those cameras also identify when you are pumping gas into a separate container. In order to identify those containers easier, federal law prohibits anyone from using non-approved containers for gas. It states this right on all gas pumps. This helps reduce the number of containers that need to be identified.

Newer cars get substantially better gas mileage than older cars. But oil companies did not want a significant drop in revenues from people using newer better gas mileage cars. Oil companies have raised gas prices. But to make up the total amount they needed to stay at the top of the income ladder, they would have had to raise prices past the rebellion point. That is the price at which people would actually take physical action against oil companies. To keep their revenues up without causing a rebellion, they went into an agreement with car companies to make smaller gas tanks but report them as larger in the car manual and on the dashboard. Gas stations were given video cameras to watch for the newer and older gas tank cars. All gas pumps were fitted with switching mechanisms to account for the type of car at the pump. Even older rotating gauge gas pumps, not just newer electronic pumps, were fitted with a mechanism to change the rate of gas being pumped to match the car's gas tank.

If you take your newer car apart and compare the actual physical size of your gas tank to an older model car's gas tank of the same stated capacity, they will look about the same, on the outside. Old gas tanks have a thin metal wall. Newer car gas tanks are made of lighter stronger material that is much thicker than old gas tanks, making the inside volume smaller by ten percent. Therefore your new gas tank looks the same on the outside but is smaller on the inside.

If you are looking forward to electric cars to get you out of this mess, know that oil companies are already working on adjusting battery sizes and capacities to short you there too.

Chapter 8
Dial Tone

The dial tone never went away. Telephones used to have a dial tone that you would hear when you picked up the phone to make a call. That dial tone is not heard on cell phones. Why not? And why is it still on regular house phones or landline phones?

That dial tone was rather loud for what was supposedly a normal background tone indicating the telephone line was available for making a call. It was called a tone, but it was not a single tone, as in a single note on a piano. If you listened closely you could tell that it was a set of sounds, but you could not determine what those sounds were. The public explanation was that it was the electric current connecting your phone to the main telephone switching office producing that sound. Why is there no sound on cell phones telling you a signal is available to a cell tower? That tone is only there on landlines before you make a call.

The truth is that tone is filled with a set of specific frequencies that send signals to your brain. Those signals are used as a testing ground for mind control experiments. Certain types of signals affect behavior or can even make a person do certain things.

In the early days of mind control experiments, it was found that certain types of sounds had predictable effects on people. But the effects were hard to pin down due to a lot of variable factors in different people. There needed to be a way to test those sounds on very large numbers of people. Telephones were just starting to be used then, but operators connected all calls. There were no dial tones. You would pick up the phone and an operator would come on the line. You would tell her who you wanted to talk to and she would connect you to that person's telephone.

The earliest designs for replacing operators had no sound when you picked up the telephone. This presented a problem when people who were accustomed to the old system would wait through the silence for an operator to come on the line, not realizing that they were supposed to dial the number themselves. The search for a solution to that problem of how to prompt people to dial a number came up in meetings of the very people who were running mind control experiments. They realized there was an opportunity to send tones to thousands of people every day, knowing it would grow into the millions very soon, to test their reactions; an almost endless supply of test subjects who would not even know they were being tested on. Plus it would be free for the people running the experiment. They proposed having a tone to prompt people to dial a telephone number, or a "dial tone". It was not called a sound or a note or even prompt. Tone is an electronic sound that can convey information. By using the word tone, they pretty much said that they are sending you information.

These experiments were not always on every dial tone on every phone in the country. The experimenters would just add their desired information to random people's dial tones whenever they wanted to run an experiment. Using thousands of available subjects, they were able to perfect their mind control tone and make people do anything they wanted within the available range of tone control. It is not all powerful, but it does affect a lot of behaviors and can be combined with priming someone to respond to certain tones to get a more precise response.

That brings us to today's cell phones. Are you safe because your cell phone has no dial tone? Not at all. One of the things discovered in those experiments was that subsonic (below what you can normally hear) and supersonic (above what you can normally hear) tones actually do a better job at mind control than sounds in the normal human hearing range. It does not take much electricity at all to make those sub and supersonic tones, which saves on cell phone batteries.

While people picking up their home phones provided short time frames each day to send out any desired tones, there was not enough time available to do any large scale control of the population in a predictable way. There needed to be a way to have those dial tones running all day long, which is exactly what a cell phone does: a phone you carry with you all day with the power on, that you leave beside your bed at night with the power on recharging for another full day of being on.

Ever wonder why your cell phone needs to be powered on all the time to receive a call? It doesn't. Your cell phone needs to be on all day so it can emit a continuous dial tone that you can't hear at sub and supersonic levels, sending out random experimental signals and specific control signals to you at any time of day or night.

Those experiments long ago on people who heard a dial tone on their phones a few times a day have now been expanded to include almost everyone, 24 hours a day, 7 days a week, without anyone knowing what is happening to them. The number and depth of experiments have increased dramatically with this new cell phone technology, allowing these experiments to refine exactly how to control people with tones. If you own a cell phone that you keep on you all the time, you are one of those being experimented on without even knowing it.

Chapter 9
Face And Body Scanners

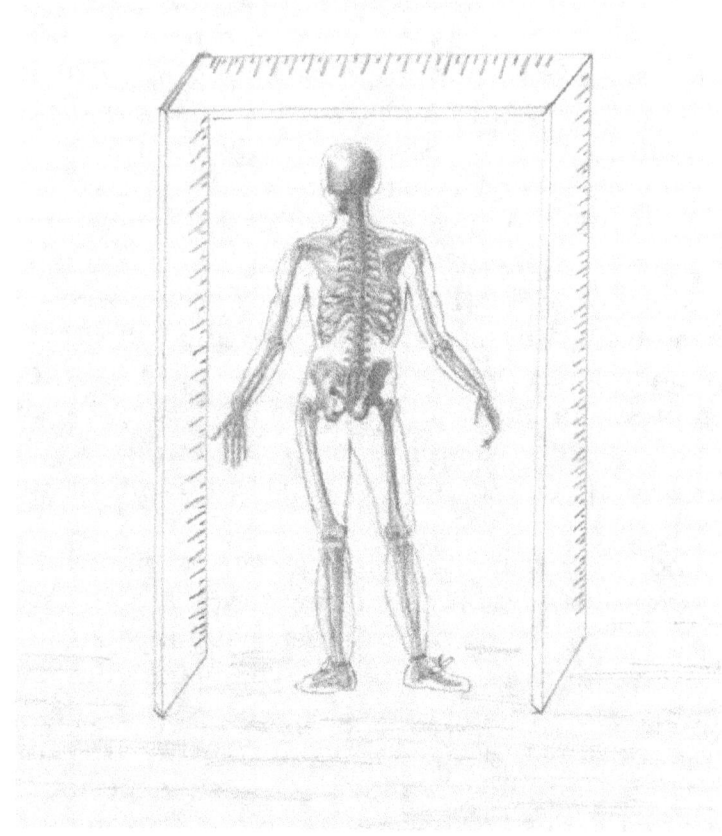

    Facial recognition systems use cameras to record people's faces then compare them to a database to come up with a match, identifying almost anyone whose face is in that database.

    Databases of faces and personal information are built up from driver's licenses, employee business IDs, school picture IDs, justice system arrest records (mug shots), and many other entities that require people to enter personal identification information along with identifying pictures.

Cameras that record faces in public are almost everywhere. Security system cameras are placed in almost all public buildings, many private businesses, and even in many private homes (nanny cams).

This is a very large infrastructure devoted to capturing face pictures to identify people. And it is all a farce.

The computer mathematical modeling to understand the difference between two faces does not work very well at all. Cameras do not capture nearly enough data points to separate one face from another. Simple variations from shadows, makeup, direction (looking up or down or sideways) and many other face changing items all combine to make it nearly impossible for computer systems to identify one face from another or to identify the same face in two different pictures.

So you would think you cannot be identified from these cameras, right?

Wrong.

All this infrastructure of cameras, databases of your information, and ID pictures does in fact do a very good job of identifying you. But they don't identify your face. They identify your limbs. Or more specifically, the pivot point distances on your body.

The problems with mathematical modeling of human faces have always been well known. While humans can recognize faces even when small changes occur, like smiling and frowning, computers still have trouble with those small changes. Very little progress has been made in overcoming those problems.

But there has long been a much easier way to mathematically model human bodies. By measuring the distance between joints on a human body, you come up with a set of numbers that are unique to each person on the planet. These are measurements from one bending point or pivot point to the next one on the human body: shoulder, elbow, wrist, knuckles, neck, spine, hips, knees, ankles, toe joints. All these combine to make a unique body signature for you. While this does change as you grow, the total dataset changes in proportion so that even if the measurements are not updated, the proportions are still consistently identifiable. The ability of computers to model these numbers is a rather easy task, and they have been able to do this for decades.

How can they use your joint distances if they only take pictures of your face in all those ID photos? Those photos capture a lot more than just your face. Next time you get one of those ID photos taken, pay attention to how far you are from the camera. It will typically be more than a few inches. At that distance those cameras can capture your whole body. They only use the small part of the photo that has your face in it to put on your ID, but they record your entire body and put that information in the database. And it is not just one ID camera taking your photo. Look around, you may see other security cameras adding more information to the full body photo they just took. That is why motor vehicle license branches always have long waits. They want you to sit down, stand up and walk to different service windows so other cameras can take better images of your joints bending to add to the database. And filling in forms by using your fingers to hold a pen makes for great finger joint measurement pictures.

License branches have been the best place for gathering your data and measuring your joint distances. But recently, newer technology has been developed to take a highly accurate picture of every joint in your body all at once: those airport full body security scanners. Those scanners are for security, just not in the way you are lead to believe. They take an almost x-ray style picture of every joint in your body with very high accuracy in just a few seconds. That scan is then added to your information in the database. While you might complain about the invasiveness of those scanners, just think about how much quicker that is than sitting around at a license branch waiting for your photo to be taken.

Then why bother with all the emphasis on face photos if they actually take body joint measurements instead? To distract you and stop you from being able to hide your identity from security cameras. If you are taking great pains to disguise your face from security cameras, all the while walking in full view of those cameras showing them your body joint dimensions, you may as well be naked with your name tattooed on your forehead.

That is why you see so much emphasis on facial recognition on TV shows and movies. They want you to believe it is your face that contains your publicly identifiable information, so you are comfortable hiding your face if you are planning anything nefarious, all the while walking with your joint distances showing in plain view. Maybe even holding a weapon with your fingers bent nicely in plain view too.

What if, God forbid, you have an accident and either break a bone that distorts your joint distances or even lose a limb? In all cases of possible bone damage or loss you go to a hospital which takes all your identifying information, then takes x-rays to get detailed images of those changes and adds that to the database of your joint dimensions, updating it with these new changes.

If you want to hide your body joints from all those cameras everywhere, try loose fitting clothing that does not show your joints: long dresses, robes, long coats, etc. The trend in the mid 1900s toward tighter clothes and shorter skirts was actually being pushed by the government to try to make people's body joints more visible in public. This has succeeded for the most part. Now anyone with long loose clothing stands out more to those watching from all those cameras. They won't be able to identify you, but they will follow you to see why you are wearing those clothes.

Chapter 10
The Hidden Internet

When you go to a website, it almost always starts with www, and ends with either .com or .org or any number of internet top-level domains. You can also start it with the usually unneeded http://. Other specific types of websites can start with ftp or other similar short intros.

But there is a hidden internet that secret government agencies use to transfer information and communicate with each other. It is hidden in plain sight, fully accessible to anyone with an internet connection. It starts with letters other than www or ftp. In fact, these hidden websites start with more than three letters, sometimes a lot more. Instead of a website name like www.easytofind.com, these hidden websites are more like fttrgh.youwontfindthis.cmuhnqq23w. The intro and ending parts are intentionally convoluted to prevent anyone from accidentally stumbling across these sites. If you accidentally add a few extra W's at the beginning of a website, you won't find the hidden ones.

Each specific secret government agency website has its own combination of intro and ending characters. Some agencies have matched the intro and ending characters to make it easier for their agents to remember: something like w34rf.secretsite.w34rf.

The usefulness of these unusual website names is that when you look at someone's history of what they typed in the web browser (assuming an agent was forgetful and did not erase his tracks), these look like random goofs, not something you would try to go look at. But if you do, you will just get a normal error page saying that site doesn't exist. Except that is not an error page, that is the intro page to the hidden website. There are several methods to get into these websites. The following are just a few examples.

Placewords

One method used by agencies is a clever security system called a placeword page. Usually to get into a secure website, you would enter a name and password. These sites offer some security. But if someone gets your password, they have access to that website and all of your information it contains. There are hacking programs that repeatedly try combinations of passwords all day and night until they hit upon the right combination of characters that happen to be your password. There are also keylogging software programs set up secretly on many computers recording every keystroke you make on the keyboard. Even secure computers used by government agencies can be compromised by these spy programs. Computers accessible by agents on secret missions can easily have spyware on them.

Those government agencies knew that agents on secret missions were vulnerable to these spy programs. Using methods other than a password to verify authorization for the secret website meant extra channels were needed for communication, which increased the complexity of missions and added ways agents could get caught. This was no way to disseminate secret information. It all had to be through the website only.

To overcome this they came up with a placeword system for passwords. A placeword is a password you have to enter on the correct place on a webpage, a non-obvious place. If you are looking at an obvious box for a name and another one for the password, that is where people (and all those hacking programs) normally enter them. But on a placeword page you would actually have to place your mouse pointer elsewhere on the page, then enter the password there. It may be on a certain letter or in a corner or on a specific part of an image. Where on the page is known only to the people authorized to use that page.

This system makes it impossible for anyone to enter your password correctly even if they know it. No matter how many times they try to enter it in the password box, it will never work, assuming there is even a spot on the webpage that looks remotely like a place to enter a password. Computer spy programs that record every keystroke you enter do not show where you entered the password. They cannot help anyone break into these secret websites.

When a government agent enters the correct and unusual website name, they get an apparent error page. They then place the mouse cursor on the correct place on the page and enter their password. Once a proper placeword has been entered and the secret website appears, it runs a program making all activity on the website invisible to the computer, as if nothing has happened since that error webpage came up. No trace of these secret websites ever remains on any web browser.

The Backspace Key

Another method used by government agencies to make it even harder for unauthorized people to access super secret websites is the backspace key. Normally the backspace key erases characters to the left of the cursor to correct a mistake when typing. Any characters entered and erased with the backspace key do not show up on whatever password you enter on normal websites.

But on certain secret websites, the backspace key is also recorded along with the character that was apparently erased.

If you enter "A B C F [Backspace] D" as a password, to anyone looking over your shoulder and to all keylogging software, it looks like you made a mistake and that your password is "A B C D". But on those secret websites, the letter F and the backspace key are both part of the password.

On Apple computer keyboards, the delete key does the same function of erasing characters to the left of the cursor. The Apple delete key is recorded the same as the backspace key on these websites. Only very high level secret websites have the capability to read the backspace key as part of the password.

Pressure Keyboards

Ever wonder why some keyboards make more click sounds than other keyboards? It is because some of them are pressure sensitive. When you press past a certain point, they click.

The interesting part is that those keyboards send a signal with each key press as to how far you pressed down. This can be used to send secret codes and enter secret passwords.

For example, if you press the letter Q down but not to the point of clicking, the keyboard sends a different signal than if you had pressed it to the clicking point. Without hitting the clicking point, you won't see anything entered on the computer screen. You could enter a password completely in "low pressure" mode (no clicks) and no one would see anything entered on screen. But all the letters you press would be sent to the program or special website you are on. Even keylogging spyware would not detect that any keys were pressed.

These keyboards are used almost exclusively in certain government installations. This is not used for agents on secret assignments because they cannot guarantee what type of keyboard they will have access to.

The purpose of pressure sensitive keyboards in these facilities is in case of incursion into the facility by any outside forces. Anyone secretly or overtly taking control of a physical computer in these facilities will not be able to enter the correct passwords and other necessary data to get control of the computer systems, even if they have all the passwords available to them.

This system also prevents any takeover of the computer systems by anyone on the internet or by wireless or any other remote means of tapping into the computer systems. All apparent visible keystrokes are only part of the needed passwords to access the data in those computers. The low pressure keystrokes that do not show up in the normal onscreen information are also needed. Remote access of these computers will never reveal this information.

The reason you have access to some keyboards like this is that in order to not arouse suspicion about these unique keyboards, those agencies put them out in the public sphere so they would seem like normal keyboards. To anyone who came across one on a computer in a restricted facility, the keyboard would seem normal. No suspicion aroused.

For any keyboard to work on a computer, a special program called a driver needs to be loaded on the computer. That driver interprets signals from the keyboard turning those signals into the letters you see on the computer screen. This is true of all computers and keyboards. The pressure sensitive keyboards have public drivers that do not interpret low pressure presses on the keys. This allows these keyboards to be used on any computer without anyone knowing the difference. But there are also secret drivers that interpret low pressure presses on the keys sending a separate set of signals to the computer and the program or website running onscreen. Because the driver on the computer is what determines whether those low pressure keystrokes are detected or not, the keyboards can be changed back and forth with public and private computers without any worries of anyone finding out that these keyboards are different. There does not need to be an additional level of security for these keyboards.

Wordpass

There is another method of getting to some secret web pages that requires an indirect route. Some secret web pages cannot be accessed directly by typing in their address in the address bar. If you do that, you will get an error page that is an actual error page. Those sites need to be accessed through another website first, which require a special entry in a special location that is very public: comments sections and forums.

From anywhere in certain comments sections and forums, if you enter a specific sentence, you will be transferred to another website, one of the secret websites. You could be writing a response to someone else posting about how they forget passwords and you type in the sentence "I cant' beleve you would forget that" with purposeful misspellings and a misplaced apostrophe. A window would then pop up with the secret website. You don't actually have to post the comment on the website. Just typing it in the section without hitting the post button will do it. That way you don't leave behind the actual phrase that leads to the secret website. But occasionally someone will hit the post button and leave the secret phrase on a webpage. A few (not most or all) apparently random comments or those that don't quite make sense are actually wordpass phrases accidentally posted on those forums or comments sections.

This is useful for agents on missions needing to access secret websites from public computers. No red flags are raised when you post a comment on an apparently bland random website. Of course once the window pops up with the secret website, the usual programs start running, leaving no trace of that secret website's session on the computer.

TriWord

In yet another method used by secret agencies to make it harder to enter their websites, they sometimes use the TriWord password system. This method makes it appear that someone is entering the wrong password when in fact they are entering parts of the correct password.

When an agent enters the first TriWord, an error page comes up saying they did not enter the correct password. This is actually the same page that comes up if someone really does enter an incorrect password. But then the agent enters the second TriWord and gets the same error page again. Then the agent enters the third TriWord and finally enters the secret website.

What happens is that the website records each of these attempts in order. If the correct three passwords are entered in order, then it allows access to the website.

If anyone were watching or recording these attempts, it would look like the agent was entering the wrong password until the last time. Then those watching would only try that last password first and get the error page. Any further attempts would result in rejection because they are not matching the three words in order. After three attempts from the same computer IP address, they would be locked out.

This also stops hacking programs which use many computers to send each password attempt from a different IP address. This is to bypass some website's security that locks out an IP address after three unsuccessful attempts at a password. Try too many wrong passwords from one computer, and you get locked out from any further attempts for 24 hours. Hacking programs try to bypass that by using a different computer IP address for each attempt. The TriWord program defeats this by requiring all three words from the same computer IP address.

For example, the TriWord could be "one more time". You would have to enter "one" and get an error page, then "more" and get another error page, then "time" and you would get through. Someone watching or recording these attempts would think the password is "time", enter that, then get an error page. But this is the first TriWord as seen by the website, so it will be wrong no matter what is entered next. Any hacking program at best would try "one" from one IP address, then "more" from another IP address, then "time" from yet another IP address. But since all three did not come from the same IP address in a row, they could never get in to the website.

These are only some of the methods used to access secret websites on the internet. Using them in combination makes it virtually impossible for anyone to get into these sites. All those spyware and hacking programs are useless in trying to compromise these websites.

This hidden internet in plain sight has been incredibly useful for a lot of agencies and agents around the world who have had to get access to needed information from an internet connection.

If by chance you do happen to stumble across one of these websites and actually attempt to enter a password, not only will your computer activity be monitored 24/7 but so will you.

Chapter 11
Traffic Sensors

Are those cameras on traffic lights making you look up to try to figure out how to hide yourself from them? Like so many other processes that The Powers That Be use to track you, those cameras are distracting you from how they are really tracking you.

Long ago, government entities started putting sensor lines in roads at intersections. Those sensors are used for detecting when vehicles are on top of them. That information is sent to computers which control the traffic signals allowing traffic to flow better. Or at least that is the explanation they tell you.

What they don't tell you is that for an even longer time, government agencies have been adding a series of raised and lowered bumps to the rims of all wheels on all cars and trucks and motorcycles. Those bumps create a unique signature on each and every rim produced.

Those bumps are extremely small and not normally noticeable. If you run your finger along the edge of a rim of a wheel, you might be able to feel slight bumps, but you would normally pass that off as just a normal variation in the metal of the rim. However, those bumps actually make up a code unique to each rim.

It is public information that road sensors pick up a metal signal from the vehicle on top of them. What is not public is that those sensors are much more sensitive than advertised. And they can pick up those slight variations in your wheel rims. That information is used to identify individual wheels on your vehicle, and thus your individual vehicle, no matter what license plate you have on your car.

Not only are those sensors located at intersections, they are placed all throughout the roadway system. The next time you drive along the road, look at those repaired cracks in the road. A lot of those supposedly random cracks seem to be rather straight across the roadway. Those are not repaired cracks; those are more road sensors, collecting information on where you are going, everywhere you drive. More accurately, where your rims are going.

One obvious question is why don't they just read the vehicle engine number, or other normal ID numbers stamped on places in a car, if those sensors are that sensitive?

There are two reasons for this. First, the early versions of this technology could only read variations in metal that was directly on top of the sensors without other metal in the way. Second, ID stamps on engines and other parts are what people will normally file off if they think those can be tracked. If you attempt to file down your tire rims, you will easily blow your tire out on the road, making the whole effort pointless.

All the ways you would normally think of to stop government agencies from tracking you do not stop them from tracking your car. You can buy license plate covers to make your plate unreadable to traffic cameras, or even steal a different plate to put on your car. That won't help. You can tint your windows to stop cameras from seeing you. That won't help. You can turn off your cell phone or leave it at home. That won't help. You can turn off all GPS devices on your car. That won't help. You can clear your car of any tracking devices that may have been placed on your car. That won't help. They will still be able to track you through the code on your rims.

You could buy new rims for your car. But the purchasing information will be used to identify that you have a new set of rim codes for your car. Even if you buy used rims from a private person, they will still be able to identify that your car has different rims, by using those traffic cameras. It is the only real use they have for those cameras: identifying what cars are driving on new or changed rims.

It might seem prudent to just get a bicycle, but those rims are marked too.

Chapter 12
LHC Black Hole

The Large Hadron Collider (LHC) is a particle accelerator that smashes atomic particles together at incredibly high speeds in order to break them apart and see what they are made of. The LHC is the world's largest and most powerful particle accelerator. People are worried that it may have produced mini black holes that have fallen to the center of the earth and are currently there, eating slowly away at the earth, which eventually will destroy the entire planet.

Mini black holes are like their larger star-sized counterparts. Large black holes are made from collapsed stars. The stars are compressed so small that gravity becomes the dominant force, making it impossible for anything to escape, even light. If the sun were compressed into a black hole, it would be a few miles wide. Mini black holes can be made from compressing very small amounts of matter, such as individual atoms, by smashing them together at very high speeds. Such mini black holes would be less than the size of an atom. They would have no more gravitational pull than an individual atom. But any atoms they came into contact with would be sucked into them, never to escape.

Physicists have stated that the LHC cannot produce mini black holes. But unfortunately, to prove their point they use a contradiction and also try to bend reality to an equation.

The Contradiction

Almost every press release about the LHC uses this contradiction to prove that there is no threat of producing a black hole.

The statement from the LHC team is this:

A) The LHC produces highly intense energies not seen since the Big Bang around 13 billion years ago.

B) Cosmic rays hitting our atmosphere produce the same energy as the LHC. If the LHC could produce black holes, they would be produced all the time over our heads from cosmic rays.

Which one is it? Does the LHC produce energy levels not seen in the last 13 billion years, or merely the same as happens every day in our atmosphere?

Look it up. They repeat this over and over again. They see nothing wrong with it. Relying on a blatant contradiction to prove that the LHC will not produce black holes is not comforting.

The Equation Over Reality

Physicist Stephen Hawking predicted that all black holes will lose mass and eventually evaporate by the following process. Virtual particle pairs pop in and out of existence from the quantum vacuum (the nothing of space). They are opposites of each other, come together and annihilate each other, then disappear from reality. Since a physics law says that mass (matter and energy) cannot be created nor destroyed, the pair that appeared out of nowhere must disappear back to nowhere to not violate this law. (Notice that we are already making actual physical objects appear and disappear to satisfy an equation.) As long as they both disappear, all is right with the universe and laws of physics.

If this happens near the edge (event horizon) of a black hole, one of the pair will be sucked into the black hole. And for some reason, it is always the negative mass one that does this, even though black holes seem to have a very consistent behavior of attracting positive mass objects to them through the black hole's intense gravity. Again, when it comes to these virtual particles, now supposedly black holes behave in the opposite way that they normally do. In so doing, attracting a negative mass object into a black hole causes its total mass to decrease, because ... it says so in the equation, even though another physics law says that mass cannot be created nor destroyed. But in order to keep consistent with that law, that second virtual particle also behaves in the opposite way all other particles do around a black hole. It takes its positive mass and accelerates away from the black hole, in the form of radiation. Thus, when you add these equations up, you get a negative mass decreasing the mass of a black hole and a positive mass escaping from the edge of a black hole. Therefore, to someone outside the black hole observing this, it appears as though that mass in the form of energy has escaped from the black hole, like pulling a piece out of it. Even though two particles suddenly appeared from nowhere and behaved in the opposite ways that all other particles behave.

If you don't mind ignoring contradictions, and believe that particles that appear from nowhere in space read earth based scientific journals, and change what they do to make sure not to upset earth based physicists, then there is no problem.

Otherwise, the mini black holes produced by the LHC are dropping into the center of the Earth and are going to end up destroying this planet.

How long do we have?

The black holes produced by the LHC are incredibly small, smaller than atoms. That means they do not have much of a gravitational pull. If you set two pencils beside each other on a desk, they have more gravitational pull toward each other than mini black holes do. Earth's gravity will pull the black holes down, all the way to the center of the earth. But because of their incredibly small size, only atoms that they literally run into along the way will be pulled into them. The amount of atoms they run into does increase as they get to the center of the earth, as densities of material increase down there.

When they get to the center of the earth, they will pass by it and go a little ways towards the other side, but not all the way. The drag of running into atoms prevent the black holes from escaping to the other side of the earth. So they will swing back and forth slowing down until they settle down into the center of the earth. The black holes will eventually merge with each other, making a larger one, which will swallow atoms that get smashed down on it. As atoms disappear into the black hole, other atoms will fill that vacuum left from the missing atoms and get sucked into the black hole too. As this happens the black hole will grow in gravitational pull, but not much in actual size. But as the gravitational pull increases, the black hole will continue to pull in more and more material, leaving bigger and bigger vacuum gaps that other earth material will fall into. This will continue until all the liquid type material in the earth's interior has fallen into the black hole. Above that, the more solid material will maintain a stable shell far enough away from the black hole to not fall into it. Think of a ping pong ball. It is stable enough that when you try to compress it by hitting it, it does not collapse.

Won't the black hole be powerful enough to overcome all resistance from that shell of solid material and send the rest of the earth crashing into it? Not really. Any black hole has the same gravitational pull as the amount of material in it, no more than that. The unusual thing about it is that a LOT of material is compressed into a very tiny space. If the earth were to be compressed into a black hole, it would fit into the size of a peanut. Even though a lot of earth's material would be sucked in, it would still only exert the gravitational attraction equal to the earth in place of the earth. You would feel the exact same gravitational pull if you were five thousand miles from the center of the regular earth as you would if you were five thousand miles from black hole peanut earth. The earth would be hollow with a black hole with about one earth mass in it, but you would not feel any different at the surface.

There are, however, side effects from this hollowing out of the earth. The biggest two are magnetic fields and heat.

With the center of the earth hollowed out, the interior metal core would no longer produce any magnetic fields. One consequence of this is that, because our magnetic field protects us from the sun's solar radiation and also cosmic rays, for a short time we would see fantastic northern lights all over the planet, a few days before we all die.

There is the possibility that the black hole would produce some sort of magnetic field. But what type, how intense, and how uniform are all unknowns. We could have a near perfect replacement of our regular magnetic field, or a crazy changing variable magnetic field, or a weaker or stronger one. Most likely though it would not be the same nor even similar enough to give us a stable cover from the sun's radiation.

All heat that was produced in the center of the earth would be gone too. Without interior heat, the planet would lose its balance of heat that has kept the surface of earth at a relatively stable temperature (even including the ice ages) that has allowed life to exist here so long. The planet would freeze, badly. Volcanoes would never be active again.

The strange thing about these effects is that they have already happened, on the planet Mars. It has lost its magnetic field and it has no interior heat, no active volcanoes even though there is evidence of previously active volcanoes. And there is a big rip on its surface that appears to be from some massive disruption of the size of the crust of the planet.

Yes, Mars is a hollow planet with a black hole in the center. How it got there is unknown. Was there a population of some intelligence on Mars that built its own LHC? We'll never know because if they were there, they did not survive the hollowing out of their planet to tell us.

Chapter 13
The Calendar

The modern calendar was designed to cheat you out of your free days each month and addict you to work.

When the modern calendar was first developed, it was originally made to give people a few extra days of rest at the end of each month, along with the days of rest on the weekends. Every month was to start with the 1st on a Sunday, which would put the 28th as the last Saturday of the month. Then the 29th, 30th and 31st were to be free days of rest and relaxation. Half the months had two extra free days (29th and 30th), half of them had three extra free days (29th, 30th and 31st). February was the only month with no extra free days, which is why every four years it would get one added to it (29th, leap day of leap year).

Each new month would start out with a Sunday the 1st. You start with one day of rest, and end the month with two or three days of special rest. The 29th, 30th, and 31st were not even given weekday designations because weekday names were for determining work days.

But those in power quickly changed that, because they did not want workers and slaves to have that time to themselves every month. They did not want people to have a predictable and patterned monthly rest schedule. They needed to keep workers and slaves off balance to be able to control them easier.

Imagine going to work knowing it will be four weeks then a break, four weeks then a break, every month, all year, every year. You would be calmer, more empowered to think of work as a set time that you deserve to have a break from. It would make you more likely to see that you can substitute the place you work at for another place if you want. You can think in terms of substituting that four week set of work with a different four week set of work. Businesses become blocks that you can change at your will, not at their will.

The mental difference of such a calendar was too empowering for the workers and even slaves when that calendar was first used. That is why it was changed to the modern calendar system of every day of every month being given a weekday work designation, with no extra days off except random holidays throughout the year. That makes workers look forward to that one day coming up in a month or two.

Many current psychological tests show that random rewards make people more addictive to those rewards, and more dependent on those who give those random rewards, than on stable timed predictable rewards. This is why people get so hooked on gambling. The randomness of the reward makes people stay and try for the next reward. This difference between stable rewards and random rewards became apparent to those in power when the modern calendar was being developed.

After the first stable calendar proved to be too empowering to the workers, several types of calendars were tested over a very long time frame to find what would keep workers working without giving up completely. Combinations of weekly and monthly days off, either random, stable, or none were experimented with. A mix of stable weekly and random monthly days off were found to be the best at keeping people addicted to work without either empowering them or breaking them completely. This, along with constantly changing the week day designations for the monthly dates, kept workers off balance just enough to be able to keep using them at will.

The modern calendar was designed to make you more psychologically dependent on business owners giving you a job rather than you having control of what jobs you want to do. It has worked for over a thousand years and continues to work today. No one will ever change it because those at the top want to keep it, and everyone else at the bottom is too addicted to the random rewards of the current calendar to give it up.

Chapter 14
Clock Numbers

Ever wonder why you look at a clock or watch when you do? All time pieces emit a small subsonic tone at the exact moment they want you to look at the numbers on the clock. Those numbers match instructions that were implanted in your brain through other means. Seeing the numbers then sets off the implanted instructions that cause you to do what The Powers That Be want. Sometimes you won't remember following the instructions. Or you will remember, but believe that you wanted to do them of your own free will. What those instructions are and what they make you do is unknown.

Occasionally an error occurs in the instruction set, and you will be stuck in a loop of looking at clocks at the same repeated time number every day, such as 11:11. When that happens, those who implant instructions will become aware of the error loop you are stuck in and take corrective action, resulting in you no longer looking at that same number time every day. You will go back to looking at a clock when the signal tells you to, following the instructions implanted in your brain.

Alarm clocks that wake you up are actually conditioning you to respond when a clock makes a sound. Every day you respond in the morning when a clock makes a sound. Then after that, you also respond when they make a subsonic sound. The conditioning of your response to an audible alarm trains you to respond to a subsonic sound.

In the old days before alarm clocks, people would get up at whatever time they needed with no alarms to wake them. There were some people who occasionally needed a prompt to wake up. But most of the population would get up at whatever necessary time without any problem. You really don't need an alarm clock to wake up, unless you have been conditioned your whole life to depend on one. If so, it is now like a drug addiction. You can't wake up on time without it. Which is exactly what The Powers That Be want: for you to be bodily physically conditioned to react to hearing a sound, even subsonic, from a clock.

This conditioning is conducted on children at all schools, public and private. All schools have clocks in the front of the classroom. When the bell rings, kids look at the clock. Kids will even look at the clock in anticipation before the bell rings. Their expectation to do something when a sound is emitted from a clock is so strong they are actually happy to anticipate and participate when that sound happens.

Some teachers put the clock on the back wall behind the students. While this would seem to be an attempt from those teachers to break students of that conditioning, they are actually increasing the conditioning by making kids look around for the clock when it makes a sound. So when kids are used for clock subsonic sound assignments, they will make sure to look around for a clock or other timepiece emitting the subsonic sound, to find those numbers that give them their assignment.

In recent years watches have been used less and less; while computers, cell phones and smart phones have been used more and more. Those who implant instructions have made sure to include a small clock on all these devices as people spend more time looking at them. These devices all have some form of alarm clock or other sound alerts to condition people to look at them when a sound is made, so they will know where to look when they hear that subsonic sound, ready for instructions in the numbers they see on that small clock on the screen.

Chapter 15
Honey Bee Robots

Honey bees were replaced by robot bees long ago. Colony collapse disorder is due to increased wireless signal interference with the robot bees electronic guidance systems.

Have you noticed that people do not get stung by bees as often as they used to? It still happens, but not as often. This is because the robot replacement bees do not sting people at random like real live bees do. When bees sting you, they leave their stinger in you. You can see the details of those stingers under a microscope. If the robot bees were to sting you, they would leave no stinger (which would be suspicious). Or if anything would be left in you, you would be able to see that is it not biological, but in fact mechanical (which would be very suspicious). You would have to look very closely though, as robot bees are made to look real at first glance, even when broken apart. If you smash one, you would not notice right away that it is a robot bee. You would have to look closely with a magnifying glass or a microscope to see that is it made up of mechanical parts.

There are still some natural bees around. But most colonies out there are mechanical robot bees. They are used for large scale surveillance of outdoor areas, where it would be too obvious to use other methods of surveillance. They can be used one at a time to track individuals, or in large groups to watch an entire area. They can even track each person in a large group of people, something that is rather difficult by other means.

Robot bees are sometimes used for injecting various poisons or inhibitors into people. These range from chemical agents that will slow a person down until they sit there unaware of what is happening to them, to agents that render a person unconscious, to lethal agents. The type just depends on the mission. All of these processes leave the person unable to remember that a bee stung them, assuming they even felt the sting at all. The injections are virtually painless. Robot bees make the injection process unnoticeable, especially when compared to having a person do the injection.

The point of these injections is to either do something to you directly, or do something to your possessions, or prevent you from interacting with someone or something for awhile. Why they do this is unknown. But if you ever find yourself having missing time, or even those times when the hour or day has gone by strangely quickly, you may have been injected by a robot bee.

When not being used for any specific mission, robot bees actually do the same job as regular bees, but not as effectively. They actually fly from plant to plant, pollinating plants like regular bees. The reason for this has to do with the history of the introduction of robot bees.

When robot bees were first developed, they would be sent out one at a time, not sent out as a whole colony. The idea back then was to put only one out on a mission to be virtually undetectable. But they ran into a problem: nature. Birds and other predators eat bees, even robot ones. And other bees will attack rivals. Some robot bees would even have mechanical problems which would result in them going down. When a robot bee would encounter any problem resulting in it not coming back to its home base, a human would have to go out and retrieve it. This defeated the whole point of using a robot bee for its stealth.

Two solutions to these problems were developed. First, to deal with the bees being eaten, most of the materials used in the robot bee were developed to break down rapidly in the presence of certain chemicals found in the digestive systems of predators. The rest of the materials will break apart easily to make very little evidence left that there was a robot bee at all, and cause no apparent harm to the predator (large die offs of predators would draw attention). Second, to increase mission success and deal with rivals, entire colonies of robot bees were set up to cover large areas exclusively for their use. But to do that meant to replace the function that those other bees were doing: pollinating. This, however, provided a cover for robot bee missions.

Pollination is a very large industry, with beekeepers taking colonies of bees to various locations across the country to pollinate crops for farmers and orchards. This happens in the U.S. and many other countries around the world. No one thinks anything when a beekeeper sets up a colony of bees in some random location out in a field or other open area. While this is a legitimate function of real live beekeeping, it is also used by a certain government agency to set up their robot bee colonies to go on missions somewhere in that region. While there, they will perform the same function as a regular colony. It would be odd if certain beekeepers kept bringing their colonies to farmland only to end up with no pollinated plants in that area.

The only problem that robot bees have is they are not good at producing honey. In fact, they don't produce it at all. While this was not a problem in the beginning, it started to become a problem as more and more regular bee hives were replaced by robot bees. In order to avoid a honey shortage, a lot of work has gone into the artificial production of honey (really a very close honey substitute). Oddly enough, for a food substitute, it is one of the most exactly matching products down to the molecular level of any artificial food out there. This was not designed for maximum dollar profit as other food substitutes are. This was designed to be an exact replacement for the food in question. It apparently has succeeded quite well. Too bad other artificially produced foods are not this good at matching what they are replacing.

While a colony of robot bees regularly pollinates the plants in the area, some of those bees are off on specific missions. They go in groups to protect and recover any bee that ends up with any problems. Robot bees can fly a lot farther and a lot faster than regular ones, making their secret mission area more than just the fields they are located in. As to what they do and who they do it to when on those missions is unknown.

Some time ago, suspicion of those bees arose in certain areas, mainly some South American countries. In order to stop any close investigation into those robot hives, a plan was devised to keep people away from bees in general. What is known as the Africanized honey bee was actually a story to scare people away from those hives. Some robot bees were made that would blatantly attack people in order to scare people away from all bees. No one wants to go looking too closely at bees that might sting you to death. They even killed some people in order to make this seem as real as possible. Killing random people in order to keep their secret is no big deal to agencies who run these types of operations. The Africanized bee story worked so well that it was decided to spread that idea as far as possible to provide a long term cover for all robot bees. They spread north to cover all of North and South America. There are even stories of such bees elsewhere in the world. Now no one wants to go poking around random bee hives due to the fear of being stung to death. This fear has kept the robot bees from being discovered.

Recently however, a problem has arisen with robot bees: they would just stop working. Random robot bees would just stop mid-flight or in the middle of a mission or even in the home base colony. This was happening to more and more robot bees. Why this was happening was partly due to the advanced electronics in robot bees.

Electronics and computers of all types are advancing in power and ability while they also become smaller. As electronic components have become smaller, they have started to run into an unusual problem: electronic interference from more and more sources. A copper wire for an old landline telephone actually has millions of copper atoms across the diameter of the wire. If a random electronic signal moves the electrons of a few of those atoms in a different direction than what the telephone conversation needs, it is not even noticeable in that conversation. But electronics have become so small that the number of atoms involved at any one point in the physical component of signal processing is now counted in the tens or ones, not millions. If a few of the electrons of those atoms are interfered with, it does make a very noticeable difference in the signal that goes through. Even mild random electronic interference can cause havoc with the intended signals.

These smaller and more vulnerable components in robot bees have been coming up against a problem in the wild: more wireless electronic signals everywhere. Increasing use of cell phones, wireless internet, digital

TV, and other electronic devices that send out radio waves have all combined to interfere with their navigation, flight and other systems, which makes them unable to operate successfully.

Losing a few bees to these signals at first was not a problem. But with the rapid increase of wireless signal pollution, enough bees are affected to become a problem with doing the public cover work of pollinating crops. Due to the needed components in robot bees, it is not possible to increase their size to make them more robust against signal interference without increasing dramatically the size of the robot bees.

What solution does the government agency in charge of the robot bees have for this problem? Currently, they don't have one. Whether they will have a technological solution or change to another device to carry out their missions or come up with something else is unknown at this point.

Chapter 16
Extra People

Look around at the next school sports event you go to. Do you personally know everyone there? Of course not. There are people from the other team there, kids from that other school, parents of those kids, and random people from your own school that you really don't know. You never really notice who is and is not there. But if you were to take each person at those events and match them to a student or teacher or staff or alumni from each school, you would end up with some extra people. At every school function those extra people are there to watch and keep tabs on how each student is reacting to that event.

You have probably heard that your school record will follow you your whole life. But when you get out of school you find it laughable that anything you do in elementary or junior high or even high school would have any influence on your adult life, outside of the one exception of high school grades getting you into college.

But there actually is a record from your school that does follow you. It is not your grades nor any behavior report. It is a report from those extra people at all those school events. They are there to watch your reaction to specific events, your compliance and your willingness to go along with the crowd or not. That is just the start of what they are measuring about you.

Those extra people will set up specific social and bio-chemical experiments to test your reactions. You might think that person walking by you on the steps in the stadium accidentally bumped you, or maybe intentionally bumped you. Whatever you think and whatever your reaction is, it is a test and your response is being monitored. What are you drinking from that open cup that you just ordered from the concession stand? Ever notice how large venue events seem to have a very high proportion of open cups of liquids they give you rather than closed cans that you need to open? This is an easy way for them to run bio-chemical experiments on you. And there is no right or wrong response to these tests. They are using your responses to set up a profile of you that actually will follow you your whole life. It will be used for determining job opportunities, but not in the way you think. Their criteria for what job you get is not based on your skills, background or ability. It is the amount of control they will need to exert over you. Will they need to put you in an office to keep you happy enough to stop you from becoming agitated with the system to the point you might start taking useful action to change it? Will a factory line job keep you worn out enough to do no more than complain about large scale governmental problems?

Those extra people at events do not measure everyone there every time. They might not even complete their set of experiments on you over the course of all those events you attend. They only need to do enough experimenting to get a good idea of how to set enough people in specific jobs to prevent large scale rebellion in the population.

However, one problem arises from having those extra people at those events. What if someone goes up to one of them and talks to them? What kind of cover story will they have? Will they keep their cover or will someone realize that person has no valid reason to be there?

In order to reduce the possibility that someone might go up and talk to those extra people, a policy was implemented to stop people from talking to those extra people. That policy has been pushed throughout every school in the land: Don't Talk To Strangers.

The Don't Talk To Strangers policy is publicly seen as a safety issue for young children. Teach them to not talk to strangers in order for them to be safe. This policy is taught in all classrooms to all schoolchildren. This lesson stays with them throughout their life.

But the real reason this is taught to children is so they do not talk to those extra people at school events. If that person is a stranger, then there is no need to talk to them, and their true purpose at that event is kept secret. They will be able to carry out their experiments and test the reactions of those they came to observe without any interference.

Chapter 17
Touchscreen Scanner

The technology for touchscreens and trackpads (phones, pads, monitors, laptop touchpads) was originally an attempt to make a fingerprint scanner that could do away with the old ink and paper method.

Fingerprinting a person consists of pressing their finger on an inkpad, rolling their finger across a piece of paper and repeating that for all of their fingers. That person would have ink on their fingers requiring some alcohol based cleaner to remove it. Those fingerprints would then be recorded into a computer database. This process means that you must have a supply of ink, paper and cleaner on hand all the time along with a scanner to enter the fingerprints into a database.

To do away with all of this, a method was developed to use a glass screen to record the image of a person's fingerprints and upload it to a database easily without any other supplies or equipment needed.

Knowing that some people who are being fingerprinted can sometimes be uncooperative, one of the requirements for this technology was that it would read a fingerprint even if the finger was swiped across the surface. In coming up with programming and screens able to do this, the developers realized that this same technology would allow someone to move images on a screen the same way they would using a mouse pointer.

Usually security technology like this would not be made available to the public. If a technology has two distinct uses, one useful for the public and one useful for private security, the security use would override the public use and the technology would be kept out of the public's hands. But when the developers pointed out that putting this technology on computers and smaller screens, especially phones, would allow the government to collect everyone's fingerprints voluntarily, the okay was given to put this out to the public.

It was first introduced on laptop touchpads that replaced the function of the mouse. After some refinement it was then introduced on touchscreen devices. Now millions of people's fingerprints are collected and analyzed every day from all sorts of touchscreens and trackpads.

But you only use the tip of one finger to swipe a touchscreen. They can't get much info from that, can they? Remember that they were trying to get uncooperative people's fingerprints. The specs for this included getting the entire fingerprint image from all fingers anywhere near the screen, not just the tip of the one touching the screen. Repeated swipes from one finger allows them to record an entire fingerprint image, along with the nearby thumb and other fingers, depending on how you swipe your touchscreen.

To make sure people use their fingers for these devices, one aspect of some touchscreen technology is temperature sensitivity. Use an object that does not rise above a certain temperature on those touchscreens and you will not be able to move or activate anything. Even if your own fingers are too cold, the touchscreen won't respond to your touch. There has been a variation on touchscreens that allow the use of a specified pen device or even a specialized glove, but these are not as responsive as screens designed for your bare fingers. All variations in touchscreen technology are designed to steer you towards using your bare fingers.

As you use that touchscreen device, your fingerprints are being recorded and sent to government databases in real time via the internet. Keep in mind, every time you swipe that screen they know exactly who you are and what you are doing.

This technology has been so successful that they extended it to computer keyboards and mice. Old keyboard keys have a rough texture on their surface.

Newer keyboard keys have a glassy smooth surface which is actually a mini touchscreen that picks up your fingerprints as you type.

The technology to pick up your fingerprints from a mouse is a little different, but comes from that same research into touchscreens. One of the avenues of research used a ball or other object the person would hold to pick up all their fingerprints at once. That research seemed to fizzle as they had to use small areas for each finger on a round object to record those fingerprints. That would require having the person place their fingers at preset locations and leave them there until the readers could record them all. That process failed the uncooperative person requirement.

However, with the other technology being used for cooperative touchscreen users, this technology was given a second look and found to be very useful for computer mice, except for one problem: when placing the fingerprint reader technology on a computer mouse, the reader sections were obviously different from the rest of the mouse. This was okay when those readers were under the mouse buttons. But that would only pick up two fingerprints at most. In order to put fingerprint readers under all five fingers, new buttons were added to the sides of computer mice and touted as newer better mice for gaming and internet use. This technology was also added to video game controllers, to capture the ever growing population of home video game players. The new buttons are small, but you end up rubbing your entire finger surface across them in the course of using the mouse or controller for any length of time. Which means they get your entire fingerprints for all of your fingers.

The newer keyboards and mice are still being introduced into public use. You have some time yet before all your internet activity is not only recorded, but traceable to you specifically as the person using the computer. You may think that you can just keep your old computer running forever to avoid having to get the new fingerprint reader technology. Unfortunately, computer companies are helping get this technology into the public by purposely outdating their current computers. They continually make new versions and stop supporting their older versions. They upgrade websites and email to the point that you have no choice but to buy a new computer (that comes with a new keyboard and mouse) in order to keep using the internet. This happens with Windows PCs, Apple computers, cell phones, pads, and other computing and communication devices. The only device currently not requiring an upgrade is the old home/landline phone. That device is rarely used by any younger person as there is no texting capability on those phones. But it does not bother the government that those devices don't have fingerprint readers, because the government has been listening to who has been talking on those phones for the last several decades. It is only the silent communication devices that need fingerprint readers, and they are all getting them.

Chapter 18
Money's Edge

You have heard endless theories about what all the printing on U.S. currency might mean: why are there Latin phrases, what is with the pyramid with the eye, etc. You also know about several methods to stop counterfeiters: the special inks used, the special paper, the strip of numbers between the front and back sides, the watermark image that can only be seen when held up to a light, etc.

But there is one item on U.S. paper currency used for distinguishing a real bill from a fake one that they don't tell you about at all: the printing on the outer edge of the paper. Not the flat edge of the front or back; the four outer edges all the way around the paper bill. You normally think of the paper bills as a flat piece of paper. But they are actually more like a small book. There is an actual outer edge all the way around the outside of those bills that has printing on it. This is used as the quickest way for a Secret Service agent to determine whether a bill is fake or not, because absolutely no counterfeiter knows about the edge printing and no counterfeiter tries to duplicate it.

On TV programs that show Secret Service agents trying to determine if a bill is fake, they always talk about the printing on the face of a bill and other methods on front and back to make counterfeiting harder, like the color that changes when viewed from different angles. But all of that is just a ruse to distract you from knowing the one quick way to determine a fake bill. The edge printing immediately determines the authenticity of U.S. paper currency.

TV programs about printing U.S. currency do not show the edge printing process. They show the bills coming off in large flat sheets, and then you see stacks of cut bills. But they don't show how they cut them and what they do next with them. It makes it all seem like they go from being cut to being stacked. But that missing intermediate step is where they add the printing around the edge.

The printing is not words. It is a series of dots that make up a code for that particular bill. Like the serial number on the front of the bill, it is unique to each bill. But it does not match the serial number on the bill. The codes do not have any relation to the serial numbers. If you figure how one set works, you will not have figured out the other set. There is a database that matches those codes to the serial numbers, in case anyone ever finally figures out how to fake the edge printing.

If you look at a stack of bills, the edge looks dark, not white. But if you look at the front and back of a bill, there appears to be no printing up to the edge, where that color would be light or white if there was no printing there. Lots of photos of stacks of bills on the internet show a nice white edge. But those are all photoshopped to remove the darker edge printing of actual bills. This is intended to stop you from seeing and wondering about the darker edges on real bills.

You cannot see edge printing with the naked eye because it is too small. But the Secret Service has handheld devices that can scan bills for edge printing. A bill inserted into the device is scanned to immediately determine whether there is any outer edge printing. It is the quickest way to determine a real bill from a fake one.

A few years ago when U.S. currency underwent a major redesign, it was supposedly because counterfeiters were getting better at duplicating the old bills. But the full background reason was that as counterfeiters got better at duplicating the front and back of bills, the Secret Service was running out of excuses as to how they spotted the fake currency.

When the Secret Service finds a counterfeit bill with those scanners, they send it to a lab for examination to find other flaws, which can be used in court as an excuse as to how they determined that it was fake. They look for any variation from an actual bill, then say that variation is what they spotted originally to know it was fake. This keeps the public in the dark about those scanners.

But as counterfeiters got better at duplicating U.S. currency, it was getting harder to convict them without being able to tell anyone in court about the edge printing. So the redesign truly was to make it harder to counterfeit, but that was just to give the Secret Service more excuses to use as to how they spotted the fake bills.

The new bills actually give you a clue about the edge printing. There is a thin strip in five dollar bills and larger denominations set between the two layers of the bills, which has the denomination repeated on it. Two layers mean you are starting to build up an outer edge. And that outer edge is where they have that secret printing.

This secret outer edge printing is also responsible for the odd and seemingly unenforced law against destroying currency. Supposedly it is against the law to destroy U.S. currency or damage it in any way. There are lots of bills floating around out there damaged in all sorts of ways, but there are not thousands of citizens sitting in jail for that destruction. Bills that are ripped and taped. Bills that are written on. Bills that have parts torn off of them. Bills that are damaged by water, other liquids, fire, etc. Bills that have been through laundry machines multiple times. All this destruction has not resulted in any mass arrests of people for damaging U.S. currency. So why does that law exist?

Because there is one and only one form of damage to a U.S. currency bill that the Secret Service cares about: if someone cuts the outer edge all the way around off of a bill, removing that edge printing. Do that, and you will be one of the few people ever convicted of destroying U.S. currency. Of course they will not tell you the true reason for your conviction, just that you damaged the currency.

This outer edge printing is also behind the standard to determine if a bill needs to be removed from circulation. It is damage to the edge printing that counts. Any other standard of damage seems to not show any consistency of what bills remain in circulation and what bills get removed. But if you look at the amount of outer edge damage, then the standard becomes clear and consistent.

The next time you are looking at the details of U.S. currency and all the things on there to make it hard to counterfeit, marvel at the extremes they went to in order to distract you from ever looking at the edge.

Chapter 19
Phone Call Location

Global Positioning System (GPS) satellites orbit the Earth sending out signals which can be picked up by any device with a compatible microchip receiver in it. Those signals tell the receiver where it is on Earth to within one foot of its location. The signals can be converted to a map or any other easy to read output with appropriate software. This has proven to be useful and convenient. The satellite signals are public; anyone can use them in any device they may want to build.

But alongside those known public signals from GPS satellites is another set of signals that are not publicly known. That second set is also used for finding locations, but in ways certain government agencies do not want you to know about. Those signals are picked up by all telephones and sent as a tone along with the voice channel, and will also find your location on earth to within one foot. Because it is sent on the voice channel, even if you record a message and send it later, they will know where you made that recording because of the tone in it.

You can be located immediately when you make a phone call from anywhere in the world on any type of phone: landline, cell, satellite, any phone. No thirty seconds needed. No tracing program needed. It does not matter how many ways you try to hide or scatter your phone call routing. Even software that changes your voice does not hide that signal.

The signal is actually combined from multiple GPS satellites. Each satellite has its own unique signal, and the area each satellite covers is also covered by at least three other GPS satellites. There is a distance based distortion in the satellite signal that gives highly accurate distance information. Multiple satellite distance distortion signals combine to make a highly accurate location tone carried in the voice channel of all phone calls on the planet.

Don't expect to be able to hear that satellite tone on your phone call. Special equipment is needed to hear it. That equipment can pick up the tone on any phone device or any recording (answering machine, voice mail, wire taps, etc). It is used whenever special agencies want to find out where a caller is. And nothing that caller can do will stop them from finding out. They will, of course, never expose how they know where that caller is. In typical fashion, if they need to locate a caller using the GPS satellite tone signal, they will then use a secondary process to expose that person's location, making it seem like the secondary publicly known process was used to locate the person, keeping their secret safe.

Attempts to distort the sound on a phone call (usually to disguise the voice of the caller) do not hide the satellite signal. Due to the fact that all possible satellite signal combinations are known, any attempt to distort the voice channel becomes very easy to clear up, using reference signals to compare to the distorted ones.

All efforts to hide the origin of a call by routing it through any number of switches and computer IP addresses and relays of every type are all in vain. It is like trying to hide the origin of a piece of mail by having it go through numerous delivery agencies, even though you have put the correct return address on the envelope. There are lots of available methods to change the voice call routing information to hide its origin. But none of them affect the voice channel information itself. That is why the GPS location signal is carried on the voice channel.

Of course you will always see these disguising techniques on TV shows and movies. Entire episodes can revolve around trying to track down a caller who uses any number of ways to hide his call: rerouting calls, hanging up before thirty seconds, etc. Those techniques do exist. But they are diversions designed to keep people from knowing just how obvious their call location always is.

Chapter 20
Soviet Union Building Plan

The Soviet Union still exists. Not just the individual countries and people that formed the Soviet Union: the actual government.

Back in the 1980s, when the Soviet Union collapsed, people everywhere wondered why. It was such a large and secretive institution, covering half the globe. And it collapsed in a day. Many explanations have been given for that sudden end. Everything from economic problems, to people wanting freedom, to external powers being just too overwhelming. But none of these reasons stand up to the numerous examples of the extremes the Soviet Union went to in the past to keep in power. It handled far worse economic conditions just fine. It tracked everyone in its sphere of influence, did not tolerate dissent, and had no problem imprisoning or killing large numbers of people if too many got belligerent. It was armed to the teeth with enough firepower to stop the U.S. and all external countries from ever attacking. Its last military campaign was trying to control Afghanistan, but pulled out of there without leaving a controlling government in place, seeming like a defeat even though the Soviet Union had enough weaponry to lay waste to that entire country. It had no problem using two processes to keep in power: control and kill.

So why did it collapse?

The answer is it didn't.

The Soviet Union government was filled with people who loved hiding themselves and controlling others. Except for the figurehead Premier, the rest of the Soviet government had no need for visibility. They liked being hidden in order to increase their ability to control those under them. It is hard for people to know how to avoid those they cannot see. And not knowing who is in the government means that you don't know who is not in the government. Is that a shop owner or a government official watching you? Is that a friendly neighbor or a spy for the government? Their invisibility allowed them to control everyone in the Soviet Union countries.

In the 1980's those in power in the Soviet Union, the most secretive society in the world, saw an opportunity to make their wildest dreams come true. They could actually hide the very existence of their government, their instruments of power and themselves, and end up controlling the entire world.

They saw the period of turmoil in the 1980s with the Afghan war and a lull in their economy (which they had no problem weathering and surviving) and realized there was an opportunity to make it look to the world like they went out of business, as if the Soviet Union no longer existed. By doing so, they could extend their control over the whole planet.

In the 1980's the Soviet Union pulled out of Afghanistan, a third world country with almost no ability to fight them, making it look like the Afghanis were too hard to control. Afterwards they went into an apparent economic downturn, in an economy run by a central authority that could change any condition of its own currency and economy at will, with no external influence to consider. Then the hard line central government officials selected an apparent moderate to be the head of their government. All these conditions set up an apparent major weakening of the Soviet system.

Almost ten years later, when the Berlin Wall was felled by people now apparently able to walk up to it from the Soviet side, no one on guard duty did anything to stop this event. Previous to this event, there were guards all along the Berlin wall on the Soviet side who would shoot anyone approaching the wall. If any of those guards did not shoot people trying to get across the wall, those guards would be shot by other guards.

They had no ability to decide who could and could not go across the wall.

The story that is told about the fall of the Berlin Wall has guards just deciding all at once not to shoot anyone anymore, apparently risking being shot themselves. But the only way that decision would have been made is if it was ordered from the top of the Soviet government. No one else in the chain of command was going to risk execution to let people start clambering over that wall.

All the conjecture and stories of that day say that the guards and administrators just suddenly decided to let people be free. Sounds nice. Not true.

When the wall came down in Berlin, it did not let freedom into the Soviet Union; it let communism out. Or more specifically, it let the Soviet Union ruling entity out into the world. A long term plan was put in motion, a plan that is still being played out to this day.

If we take a look back in time to the 1950s, people in the U.S. were in a Cold War with the Soviet Union and were wary of communist spies. There were rather effective programs for weeding out possible spies in government offices and other power positions in the U.S. The Soviet Union wanted to plant long term moles in those positions, but needed to stop or greatly reduce the effectiveness of these anti-spy programs. So they used one of their more successful moles to make the process of going after spies much more difficult. They had Senator Joseph McCarthy use a psychological trick on the U.S. He went so ridiculously overboard publicly tracking down communists that eventually everyone got sick of him.

The normal history of that era states that Joseph McCarthy was so vindictive in his witch hunt of communist spies that he just went too far. Eventually, people realized he was inventing enemies to make himself look good in comparison. This could have been true. Except that a notable problem with McCarthy's public claims about the number of communists is that he was always changing those numbers. To anyone paying the slightest bit of attention, it was clearly apparent that he was just making the whole thing up, and being as obvious as possible about it too.

In the public hearings to hunt down the communists, McCarthy pushed people to get as many random names of other supposed communists as possible. This process would obviously result in innocent people being labeled as spies; a lot of innocent people. The only possible result was that he would hit a tipping point and turn the majority of people against him.

But it was not enough just to have a lot of people turn against him. Those people had to be able to tell everyone in the country of the injustice of these witch hunts. They had to have a way of publicizing their plight. That is why Joseph McCarthy zeroed in on Hollywood as his main target. There was not another group of people who had more access to publicizing the injustice of the communist witch hunts than those in the TV and movie industries. This assured that when McCarthy pushed past the tipping point, everyone in America would know how wrong it was to pursue communists. And programs that were actually doing a good job of weeding out communists in government would come to a crashing halt.

This whole process was set up from the beginning to be a big public spectacular failure, and make it a lot harder for the earlier established legitimate anti-spy programs to continue. Joseph McCarthy was working for the Soviet Union to reduce the effectiveness of anti-spy programs in the U.S. He succeeded spectacularly.

The end result was that the Soviet Union was able to plant many long term moles in several positions, both political and private, to be ready when the day came to control the U.S. That day has come.

With the apparent collapse and end of the Soviet government in the early 1990s, the U.S. let its guard down and allowed a lot of people from the former Soviet countries to have open access to levels of power, both governmental and private. They also let their guard down in one other important area: former Soviet enemies like Afghanistan.

When the Soviet Union invaded Afghanistan, they set up a plan to eventually attack and take over the U.S., but not in the traditional sense.

When they invaded Afghanistan, they ran into some small opposition, but not enough to make the Soviets flee. That opposition group did not like the Soviets, but they hated the U.S. even more. That group was the Taliban. They were not the most technologically proficient group in the world, but they were willing to get killed fighting their enemies. The Soviets gave them an opportunity to do just that.

The Soviets were devising a long term plan to take over the U.S. The Taliban fit in with their plans perfectly. They had the Taliban appear friendly to the U.S. and carry out attacks against the Soviets in Afghanistan. The Soviets had no problem sacrificing large numbers of their soldiers to carry out this ruse. The Taliban used this opportunity to learn about Americans: how to speak English, how to blend in socially living in the U.S., and how to use American schools to learn to fly American planes.

Many people believe that Osama Bin Laden was the mastermind behind the attacks on the U.S. in 2001. He was a major financial sponsor but not the creator of the plan. He is on tape saying how surprised he was that the planes actually made the twin towers collapse. Everyone was surprised that those planes made the twin towers collapse. Everyone except the Soviets.

The Soviets were known for their robust manufacturing processes. The items and structures they built were incredibly durable. The AK-47 is famous for its ability to withstand the toughest conditions and keep on working. The MiG fighter planes could take off and land on almost any solid or even semi-solid ground. Compare that to the U.S. F-series fighter jets: U.S. pilots and ground crews would regularly walk landing strips to pick up the smallest objects to make sure they did not disturb the jets as they took off and landed. The U.S. lost a space shuttle due to problems with external foam. The Soviet Mir space station caught on fire in space three times and kept going. The Soviets built things very tough compared to the U.S. And they knew it.

The Soviets had long known that U.S. manufacturing and building processes were rather fragile and not up to advertised standards. They knew the twin towers (and other U.S. skyscrapers) were unable to withstand the forces that were claimed in their blueprints. The Soviets had been paying attention to the differences in the durability and reliability of all those items discussed above, and in many other items, including the strength of the steel I-beams used in many U.S. skyscrapers. The Soviets knew what so many other people did not; that if hit by a large jetliner filled with fuel, those I-beams would melt, buckle, and break causing a catastrophic collapse. All the data and blueprint information claimed that in such a scenario, those I-beams and those buildings would survive intact. Overestimating that strength was par for the course in the U.S.

Had those buildings survived relatively intact (except for impact and burn damage) it would have been harder for the people of the U.S. to give up their freedom for security. They would have thought that they were relatively okay the way they were, able to survive such rather insane attacks. They still would have gone after the Taliban and their cohorts. But they would not have accepted severe security and monitoring intrusions into their daily lives. The buildings had to come down for that. The Soviet plan to accomplish this became known as "The Building Plan." That name had a double meaning. First was the plan of bringing down those buildings. The second was the building up of a security state in the U.S.

Think of what happened after the Oklahoma City bombing in 1995 that took down part of a very large building killing hundreds of people. Certainly people in the U.S. were horrified. But no one was willing to go into a severe security state to stop this from happening again. It was not enough of an emotional impact to make people in the U.S. compliant to a security state.

The Soviets were aware that whatever attack happened, it had to happen live on TV, and be as long and drawn out as possible. The idea of hitting both of the twin towers with a slow burn collapse was just the thing they needed. They knew the news would be watching the first tower after it was hit. They knew everyone in the U.S. would be watching the news after the second tower was hit, and would not be able to turn away from their TVs after the first tower fell, knowing that it was only a matter of time before the second one fell. This would have the largest emotional impact of any attack in history on people not directly in the line of fire of an attack. The very thing that would beat an entire population into accepting whatever security state their government wanted to put in place, whatever security state the invisible Soviet Union wanted to put in place.

There is one other problem often discussed about those attacks. How did those people learn to fly those planes so well so quickly? Many have suggested that no one can learn to fly a jumbo jet in a couple months in a flight simulator. Actually, you can. Flying in good weather is not that hard, even flying a large jumbo jet. Taking off, landing, flying in bad weather and dealing with technical problems are the hard parts.

But within the question of flying ability is a question no one has asked. How did those people know to push the engines to full throttle while flying into those buildings, but not on the way *to* those buildings? You would think that once those planes were commandeered by those people, they would just push it as fast as possible all the way to their targets. But they didn't. They knew the engines would not last at full throttle that long. However, they would last at full throttle for the short run into those buildings, running the engines over their rated capacity. How did they know how long they could and could not run the engines of a jumbo jet over rated capacity without blowing the engines? They do not teach over limit capacity in any flight school. They do not learn that reading books in the desert.

There was one group who studied this very type of thing about all jets produced by the U.S. to learn the exact limits those jets were capable of: the Soviet Union. They had the knowhow to tell those terrorists exactly how long they could and could not run those engines at full throttle before going over their rated capacity. Even the manufacturers did not know for sure how long their own jets would last at over capacity full throttle in real world flying. The Soviets studied and tried this out on all U.S. jet models in real world flying tests for their war plans, to figure out how well every single one would do in a full air war scenario. While they never used this information for an actual air war, it came in handy for a sock puppet attack on the U.S.

In 2001, a surprise attack took place against the U.S. from Afghanistan. The actual physical damage to the U.S. was not enough to do any serious long term damage economically or militarily by itself. But it did open the door for well placed people in government and private sector positions to step in and start a process to monitor and control the citizens of the U.S. While differing sides within the U.S. thrashed out theories as to why the attack happened and argued the processes that were put in place afterwards as security measures, no one bothered to look at the deep sources of the people and companies that were in charge of their implementation. No one noticed that the security measures put in place not only seemed like old Soviet Union tactics, they actually were old Soviet Union tactics: secret prisons, secret trials, torture, secret laws, mandatory IDs for traveling into friendly neighboring countries, travel bans on select individuals, cameras monitoring public places, recording communications of everyone in the country without any oversight or acknowledgment to any public agency or other branch of government, more direct control of economic processes, public pressure to support the government or be labeled a traitor, less investigations and reporting by the press, more integration of the press into military actions with a resulting support for all military actions, less diversity and more centralized control of different branches of the economy by larger entities. The question is who is controlling those entities?

The Soviet Union became invisible, attacked and restructured the U.S. (still ongoing) and other major industrialized nations (see England), and is poised to have control over everyone in the entire world, all without waging a world war or firing a shot of their own, and with no one even knowing they exist to try to stop them.

Chapter 21
Noise Canceling Bugs

If you turn up a stereo or TV really loud to hide your whispered conversation from any possible listening devices like in the movies, those who are bugging you will still hear every word you say perfectly well.

All modern bugging (eavesdropping) devices have noise canceling technology built in. This technology can take any source of sound, such as your stereo or TV, and set up an exactly matching opposing set of sound waves, to cancel that source of sound down to silence on the sound analyzing equipment they use to listen to you. Turning up your TV as loud as possible still makes the room completely silent to the listening device that is now ready to hear every whisper you make.

Bugging devices have been using this technology for several decades. Agencies that have been listening to people around the world have been able to cancel out electronic sources of sound, making rooms silent except for the people talking. In order to encourage people to feel comfortable speaking to each other about whatever secrets they had, these agencies had scenes added in movies where people would turn up radios or TVs to drown out their conversation so that others who were bugging them could not hear their conversation. This psychological trick worked. Many people who were being bugged would use this technique that they saw in the movies, turning up the volume their electronic devices to then have a whispered conversation "safe" from being heard. But all the while every whisper has been heard clearly.

However, there is a flaw in this noise canceling process. There is a way you can actually hide your conversations from those noise canceling bugging devices. The bugging devices automatically cancel out all sounds that come from certain electronic sources:

TVs, radios, stereos, and a few others that always play sounds that are not original live voices from within the rooms they are located in. Normally this ensures that no matter what noise source you turn on, the room is still essentially silent to those bugging devices. But if you can send your voice through those noise sources - a stereo or a radio - those listening devices will cancel out your voice too, and they will hear nothing. Setting up a microphone system to send what you say through your radio speakers will make your voice one of the canceled set of noises, and they will hear nothing from you at all. You can then speak freely and those who are trying to listen to you will hear nothing. Just make sure that you are not being watched when you do this so they are not alerted to what is happening.

This flaw in their bugging process was actually exploited in the 1980s. A product was sold through television commercials that allowed you to send your voice through a radio (one of the noise canceled sources). It was called "Mr. Microphone". The reason those commercials were so cheesy was to throw off any suspicion that this device was being used for a very serious purpose. It is not known what group was behind the invention and distribution of this device. The sales outlets, manufacturers, etc. were all legitimate business who knew nothing about the true use of this product. But who actually set all that in motion is not known. What is known is they found a way to circumvent the bugging equipment, and got that device out to all their members without arousing suspicion. Having this particular device show up only in those homes and businesses of this group would arouse suspicion. But by making it a popular product that was in a lot of homes and businesses, none of the bugging agencies were any the wiser.

Mr. Microphone was actually a serious anti-bugging device being distributed to a certain group that was being bugged by the U.S. government. And this was done right under the government's nose.

The government agents did not catch on to this because the computer and electronics people who created the noise canceling devices were not field agents, and did not know agents were bugging houses that had Mr. Microphone in them. The field agents were not aware of the details of how the noise canceling device worked, and did not think it important to inform the computer and electronics people back at the office that Mr. Microphone was being used in the locations they were bugging. This hole in the spying process let the Mr. Microphone device continue to be used for decades without those spy agencies discovering its true use. Due to the nature of the source of this information, it is not known whether those agencies currently know this or not.

Chapter 22
The Backtrack Program

Massive amounts of data are collected every day by the government. Every phone call, every email, all websites you go to and what you click on there, what you watch on TV, what you buy, how you react to certain situations, where you go, etc. That's a lot of data every single day.

Ever wonder how the government can go through all that data they collect on every person to find out who is a threat to them? The answer is they don't.

While they actually do a little proactive searching for information to try to get ahead of some types of threats, mostly they just wait until someone becomes a problem, then go look at all the data collected on that person, their associations, contacts and relations going backwards from the point of when that person first became a problem. This is called the "Backtrack Program".

There are two parts to the Backtrack Program: inside and outside.

The inside part consists of data collected from electronic and personal means: phone calls, emails, internet usage, financial records, known associates, TV watching habits, recordings from listening devices, etc. This data tells a lot about what you do and who you interact with. But it does not tell everything about you.

The outside part is data from satellite coverage and other video coverage. Satellites take pictures continuously of all activity on every square foot of earth every day, down to a detail close enough to read what book you are reading. They combine that with video camera coverage from local cameras located in stores and on streets to get a detailed look at where you go and what you do.

The satellite data is like a huge map of earth. To see the detail of a specific spot, simply zoom in to that one location, similar to what can be done on Google maps satellite view, but with video added that can run forward or backward starting at that location on any specific date and time. All they have to do is find a location you are at on a known date and time, identify you from their satellite views, then run that data backwards and forward from that point combined with local video footage to see where you have been, what you have been doing, who you talked to, etc. It is basically a video of your entire life. How far back in your life they can go and what detail they can see from those satellite views depends on the level of technology in use at the time.

Satellite views of earth have become better and better over time. Every time there is a major advance in imaging technology, another set of satellites are launched. It is not known when they had detailed views of everyone on earth or when this program started. What *is* known is this started far longer ago than the general public would realize.

Before satellite technology became available, hot air balloons were used for watching people on the ground far below. The earliest versions of these were obvious to people on the ground, as they would see these big balloons up in the air with people in it looking down. But better balloon technology allowed balloons to go higher and higher. Adding to that was the increase in camera technology. Cameras were starting to take pictures automatically. Film cameras were becoming hardier at operating in all sorts of temperatures and weather. Better resolution of images farther away was increasing at a rapid pace in still cameras and film.

These technological increases resulted in what we now know as weather balloons. These balloons were launched high into the stratosphere, where no one could even see them. While some weather balloons were used for their stated purpose of scientific research, other weather balloons were fitted with incredibly high resolution cameras (still pictures and film) to monitor what people were doing on the ground: people who could not even see those balloons that were high in the sky.

Records of this monitoring are cataloged and stored in large data vaults, and have long since been digitized to be able to run on computers for quick access. Pretty much every living person has their entire life of activity on visual recordings in secret data warehouses, now available to certain government agencies who can see everyone they ever interacted with and everything they've ever done. The inside electronic data tracking is not quite as detailed if you go back far enough for the oldest living people. But oddly enough, the oldest living people did a lot more activity outdoors in their early years than younger people do. Therefore, the outside data becomes more relevant when backtracking older people.

All this combined data basically becomes a recording of your entire life for certain government agencies to view at will if you ever become a problem to them. All they need is any one location you were at, which they already have, and your life becomes an open book for them.

Chapter 23
Leftover Codes In The English Language

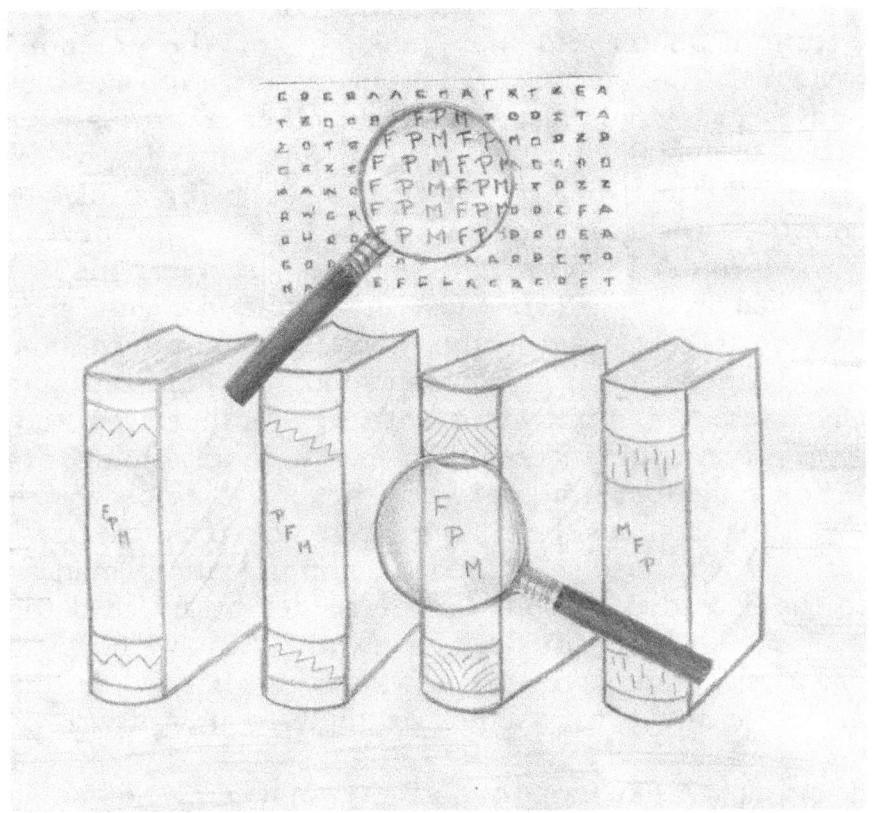

The English language is filled with words that do not sound the same way that they are spelled. Some are not even close. How did a language end up with a spelling system that does not match its sounds? Because in its early development, hidden codes were used in words that made their way into the permanent language, codes that are still in use today.

In the early years of all languages, within any era, a generally accepted set of words were used in written communication, usually defined by the current ruler of the country. Only select people (the rich, the royals, the religious, and the rulers) were allowed to read and write the language.

Sometimes writing was used to communicate to others far away. But some of those written communications did not make it to the intended audience. This became very problematic in times of war, and even in times of peace, when other countries were planning your demise. Having all your important information intercepted and read by opposing armies or countries was a big problem.

In order to avoid having all your secret plans laid bare before your enemies in writing, codes were developed to be used in those written communications. Early codes were not sophisticated, because the elite who were communicating with each other were not always very sophisticated themselves. Simple changes to words sometimes indicated that a word was not what it meant. Sometimes the changes were not so simple.

When those secret coded communications made it to the intended person, a code reader would read the message. The code reader would know how to pronounce the words, and what the changed letters meant in those words. For example, if it was written that a leader had a "coff" he could be sick and weak, but if it was written that he had a "cough" may not be so weak after all. A substitution like this may seem obvious at first glance. But consider that in the early days of language, there were no authoritarian dictionaries to set the spelling and meaning of every word in stone. So when enemies that spoke another language intercepted a coded writing, they could not be one hundred percent certain that those words were actually not the correct spelling.

There are three ways that coded words crept into the language:

From The Top Down

Beyond the ruling elite using the language in writing, the general population of the lower classes spoke that language too. Some of the lower classes would work in upper classes houses, businesses and government institutions. Sometimes workers in the house where coded messages were read would listen in on those codes and even see and write down some of those coded words. Then they would let their friends and families know of those new words along with their apparent meaning from what they heard. It was very exciting to be able to tell others of a new word in the language. Those words spread like wildfire throughout the country entering the speech of the general population. This process added quite a few code words to English (and other languages too).

From The Bottom Up

Enemies of the state were not the only ones intercepting those written communications. Local bandits would attack those traveling with secret communications: not for the communications, but for whatever valuables they could get. But as bandits got their hands on those written communications, they would study them to try to learn the secrets of writing. This was the language they spoke. They knew writing was important and here they had samples of those writings. Some writing took place secretly amongst the lower classes: they strived to match the writing used by those in power, the official writers of the language. Those coded words would spread throughout the land amongst the lower classes. Some amongst the lower classes would work for, or be slaves of, the higher classes working in their households and offices. As is now the case in many businesses and governments, those in charge would not always know as much as they claimed. They would use lower class employees or slaves to help with writing, even though they were not supposed to. An upper class government official who was charged with writing official communications would sometimes ask a lower class employee or slave about spellings of words they were not sure of. In this way coded words would work their way from stolen coded messages to the general population to official communications as legitimate spellings of words.

And Sideways

Ineptitude also played a part in coded words becoming official popular spellings. The officials who received a coded communication would not know the correct spelling of everything written in that communication. They would mistake some coded words as legitimate and start using those misspellings as official spellings.

One of the most glaring examples of code words in English are the numbers one and two. These were of course won and tue, or mon and tue as in Monday and Tuesday. Someone coded their numbers (for military or financial reasons) as one and two, switching the letters around. Since these were the first numbers in counting, the lower classes thought they hit the jackpot of understanding numbers: the beginning of numbers. These coded words went viral and stuck. But it is still obvious to this day that the letters in the words for these numbers were switched around. To this day we still refuse to change them back to their earlier correct spelling.

At some point along the history of coded words making their way into English, an official dictionary was published that cemented all the words as they were spelled at that time into the language forever. While this prevented more coded words from making their way into the English language, it unfortunately locked in the coded word misspellings in use at that time.

Different countries made dictionaries at different points in the development of their language. Ones that started earlier in their development reduced the introduction of coded words. Others that went through a more vigorous vetting of words would end up weeding out a lot of coded words. English apparently had a very late dictionary and not a very thorough vetting process, leaving it as one of the most complex spelling-to-sound systems on the planet.

The reason you are not told of this coding is because this process is still in use today, but to a much lesser extent. The advantage of this type of typo code is that people are not looking for it. They are looking for an entire document of random letters, or the starting letter in a set of words. They completely overlook some typos in a document.

When you see an apparent typo in an official writing, like a newspaper or book, or in any government communication, it is more than likely a code being used. What that code is and what it is used for, who knows.

Chapter 24
The Computer Monitor

Flat panel televisions and computer monitors (LCD/LED) are designed to be thinner and lighter than the old big thick cathode ray tube (CRT) televisions and monitors. But look closely at those screens and you will see more than just the image they are showing you.

If you were to look through a magnifying glass at an old CRT screen you would see a series of colored circles. Those are the pixels or dots that make up the TV picture. There is a similar setup on flat panel LCD monitors. Looking at those screens with a magnifying glass, you can see a bunch a squares or rectangles of color in a grid pattern. Those are also the pixels that make up the image you see.

But if you look closely at an LCD monitor you will notice the grid pattern itself, black lines that are apparently empty spaces between those colored squares. Those empty spaces are actually photo sensors. They are the same type of sensors found in modern digital cameras, but just spread out farther. They are not cameras or lenses themselves, but achieve the same result.

Digital cameras make a picture from light hitting a set of photo sensors squeezed together on a sensor chip. The lens of the camera focuses light onto those sensors which creates the image you see from the camera.

But with certain software programs you can spread out those same individual sensors without a lens and still get a coherent image from the light that reaches them. This is the same technology used on the Hubble Space Telescope. The first images from the Hubble were very blurry because the telescope mirror was not smooth and did not focus light onto the sensors correctly. They could not replace the mirror. So they came up with a way to take the blurry image and use software to rearrange the information of all that light gathered on all those sensors into a coherent sharp image. They use a far more sophisticated form of that software to obtain an image from the spread out photo sensors in your TV and computer screens. Those dark lines of the grid patterns are sensors picking up your image without a focusing lens, recording everything that goes on in front of your TV and computer. All of that image information is then sent to secret agencies.

How does that data get sent to those agencies? By any one of several methods, depending on how your television receives signals and how you are connected to the internet. Basically, they use the same process that transmits signals and information to you to retrieve information from you. So if your computer is on a telephone line DSL internet connection, that same method is used to upload your data and images back to those government agencies.

This is why your internet company always gives you a package deal of a large download bandwidth but a much smaller upload bandwidth. The available upload bandwidth is actually equal to the download bandwidth, but most of it is being used for uploading images of you in front of your computer and TV.

There is an apparently valid reason to justify the difference in upload versus download bandwidth. When you are on the internet and click on a website link, you are sending a very small amount of data to the website to request that web page. However, all of that information on a website, plus any music and video, results in tremendous amounts of data going from the website to your computer. Your internet company offers an internet deal of a smaller upload bandwidth than download for supposedly this very reason. This apparently leaves a very large imbalance of uploaded data versus downloaded data. But in fact, the upload capacity is used almost completely with the image data from your television and computer monitors going from your home to those government agency computers. This is why your internet company will only allow you a lower limit upload capacity. They do not want you to possibly attempt to saturate your upload capacity and block all that image data from getting through.

How this image upload can happen is somewhat obvious over cable, satellite and telephone lines. They transmit data both ways for internet, and can easily do the same thing with television. But how does this happen for over the air television?

For broadcast TV stations, your image data is also sent back along those same airwaves. The antenna that picks up local TV signals can also transmit on those same airwave spectrums. This has actually been done almost since the first televisions were in use several decades ago. But how did those old big curved CRT screens get your image if they weren't using modern photo sensors?

The televisions back then all used big cathode ray tubes (CRTs), with the curved screen and the big box shape. They sometimes called those big thick CRT TVs "monitors", as in "monitoring you in your house" (those spy agencies often like to clue you in to what they are doing). They used a technology similar to regular cameras back then, which is why the screens were curved. They had to act like a camera lens to capture your image. Think of the fact that movie screens were always flat, but they claimed television screens had to be curved. The claim of the necessity of a curved screen was all just a ruse to get a camera-like lens into your home and facing you from a wall. The best place to see the most activity of a family was from a wall in a highly used room, which is exactly where people put television sets.

The Cathode Ray Tube part of the television would send program images to the curved screen from inside the TV, resulting in a series of colored dots on the screen that formed the images people saw. But images received from in front of that same curved screen were focused onto a receiver inside the TV. All of that equipment took up a lot of room and weighed a lot, which is why the CRT TVs were so big and heavy. Then the receiver sent those images as a signal to the same television broadcast station that was sending out the TV programs.

Television station broadcast and receiver equipment could not handle a lot of individual signals coming in all at once. So the television sets had a built in delay to send those household images at certain set intervals. They even sent signals after the television was turned off.

There is a piece of equipment called a capacitor in old CRT TVs. Those capacitors would carry a warning that they still hold an electric charge after the television is turned off and unplugged. Why would they build it that way? To make sure there was enough electricity to power the transmission of image data stored all day back to those same television stations overnight and then on to government agencies.

As more and more people had televisions, and more than one television per house was becoming the norm, saturation of the airwaves became a problem. So a new TV broadcast spectrum was introduced.

The first television sets picked up (and sent) signals over the air in what is called a UHF spectrum, for Ultra High Frequency. A simple wire antenna on top of the television picked up those signals sent from local broadcast stations, and sent images back too. After that, a newer technology using VHF, for Very High Frequency, was used. This increased the ability of TV stations to send, and more importantly receive, signals sent over the airwaves, especially with the ever increasing numbers of home television sets.

Cable lines and satellites were then used for TV signal transmission. With that technology came the switch from analog (UHF and VHF) to digital signals. This meant broadcast stations had to have equipment for both types of signals, which was redundant and expensive. The recent requirement to go all digital over the air, replacing analog, was for consolidating TV station equipment technology instead of using a mishmash of different receiver types trying to integrate all of that data on a daily basis.

Now all of those images of you in front of your television and computer are digitally received and stored in large computer data warehouses, monitoring what you do in your home every day. For the government, you are viewed more often than any celebrity out there.

Chapter 25
Bird Flu

Each year the government announces that a new strain of bird flu is infecting people. They give this strain a number and tell everyone to get a new flu shot to combat it. And each year a lot of people speak out against getting this flu shot for various reasons but mostly because those people do not trust the government.

The government however is actually using the bird flu to flush out people who challenge government statements. As new flu strains are announced each year, troublemakers are identified when they post, email, call, write and speak out against the bird flu scares. The different bird flu strain numbers are entered into a database as data tracking numbers that compare communications from year to year, to help the government track down the main sources of non-compliant agitators.

While there are all sorts of tracking methods for finding troublemakers, the bird flu offers a unique way for government agency statisticians to use modern mathematical processes to track troublemakers from year to year. It is used as an experiment for improving models of crowd control, finding problematic people within crowds, and seeing how those people propagate problems and resistance to government directives throughout populations. Those bird flu strain numbers are an important part of the computer models that track the agitators. The crowd control models based on the bird flu scares are then applied to other situations where the government wants to control large groups of people.

The bird flu also encourages people to get flu shots every year. This allows the government to inject bio-agents into specific people in the population, testing them on a large scale. Only a small percentage of the flu shots contain that year's bio-agents. And some of those bio-agent recipients are the ones that just happen to die from the flu shots each year. The government takes those bodies to analyze how the bio-agents interact with the human body.

It is the perfect cover for these experiments. If they injected only the people they wanted to test, then a large percentage of the injected people dying would become obvious to everyone, creating problems with covering up these experiments. People would also be less willing to get these shots after seeing this outcome. But by injecting millions of people and only testing a few hundred, no one thinks anything odd about it when such a small percentage of people die from these injections. Even if all the test subjects die, it is still such a small percentage of people injected that it is statistically acceptable and no one notices.

This flu appears out of nowhere, or out of birds, or out of pigs, or out of whatever place or animal the government decides. And each year it is a new strain of flu, not like any previous flu before that, requiring everyone to get a new anti-virus injection. Sounds legit … or not.

What other disease have you ever heard of that has a completely new strain or form each year like clockwork requiring a completely new round of drugs to treat?

Even if you agree with the idea that this flu can mutate into a new version of itself each year, why only one mutation? Wouldn't there be several types of mutations that develop continuously? Why would a virus make one and only one change each year? Is there a committee of viruses that gets together annually to vote on which single mutation they will have? No, of course not. Viruses don't behave that way. But humans do. Specific groups of humans do get together to decide what biological agent will be tested on small group of people. And if you are not in the deciding group, you are likely to end up in the testing group.

Chapter 26
Transfer Pi

Want to transfer money electronically without any government agency tracking your transfer? Transfer Pi.

Long ago, when secret agents started to be used for deep cover operations, a problem arose. Some agents needed to have fast access to large amounts of cash. But other government agencies that were not privy to the secret missions were flagging those transactions. Sometimes this resulted in exposing those missions to the very governments that were being spied upon.

So how do you give secret agents fast access to cash needed without tipping off unrelated agencies? Carrying large sums of cash was too risky. Trying to inform every tracking agency of those missions was giving out too much information to too many people, risking double agents from other countries finding out about those missions. Secret accounts did not stop the tracking of large transfers from taking place.

The idea was finally hit upon to let transactions of a certain numeric value go without being flagged by any agency. But what number? Those agents needed all sorts of various amounts of cash. The more numbers you allowed to go unmonitored, the more transactions by regular people that you wanted to monitor would be going by unnoticed. Having to remember a lot of numbers was adding too much information for secret agents to deal with on top of everything else they were doing.

The solution they decided upon was to use Pi: the number that is the ratio of a circle's circumference to its diameter. 3.1415926535 is the start of it. It goes on forever. Using that sequence of numbers in any transfer of money is ignored by all monitoring systems, along with the subsequent transaction between the same accounts.

Secret agents can transfer any amount that use the number Pi from the start if they want the transaction to be ignored by monitoring agencies: $3.14 or $31.41 or $314.15 or $3141.59, etc. For example, if you transfer $314,159.26 this large of a transfer would usually be flagged for tracking. But it is in fact completely ignored by all monitoring systems. You will still see that transfer show up on a bank statement. But the automatic flagging systems that warn banks and agencies of large transfers will not see it at all.

If you wanted to transfer $100,000.00, you would transfer $31,415.92 first, then because the subsequent transfer between the same two accounts is also ignored, you would transfer the difference from $100,000.00 which is $68,584.08.

You can transfer that number in any currency since it is ignored in all tracking systems around the globe. The programming part that ignores that number was built into the very earliest banking systems and has been a basic integral part of all subsequent bank tracking systems.

Bank transfer tracking systems are built on a set of standard rules that all banks use. It is a rather large and very old set of rules and regulations that has been written into programming code, which is used as the basis of all bank transfer tracking systems worldwide.

Trying to understand a set of rules from the programming code is an extremely difficult proposition. Programming code can be very obscure when compared to the written rules it is implementing. Good programming code will have clear notes beside each section to explain what it does. This, however, is rarely done. Bank transfer tracking systems are one example of programming code that is not noted well.

Different countries have their own extra rules for tracking bank transfers. But those rules are added to the original programming. If a country wants to cancel some rule for their own regulations, new code is added to cancel that old code when it is used, instead of removing the section to be canceled. Removing old code can have unintended consequences, and most programmers try to avoid that process if at all possible, especially if the program is not noted well.

Buried deep in the original programming code base are a few lines that are not on the original rule set and do not appear to have a traceable origin. The code looks obscure, and what it does is not apparent at first glance. It cancels flagging for a certain obscure mathematical calculation in all transfers. If anyone were to figure out that obscure mathematical calculation, they would find that it equals Pi.

The simplest thing about using Pi for money transfers is that all you need to remember is Pi, not the number itself. If you forget the actual number, anybody with basic math knowledge can tell you it, or you can look it up easily no matter where you are. This is what has made it so easy and useful for agents on missions all over the world.

Chapter 27
Metal Turnstile Gates

Ever wonder why those metal turnstile gates are at all entrances through which large groups of people must pass (school football fields, park entrances, subways, movie theaters, stadiums, etc)?

Those metal bars on those gates are not empty. There is equipment in them that scans each person that walks through. That is why the bars are spaced apart as they are. It is also why they are made of metal. When you touch them, even with gloves on, the equipment in the metal generates an electro-magnetic field that detects the electrical potential across your body, which completes a circuit. The older technology of electro-magnetic field scanning required larger areas of metal. That is why older turnstile gates are larger. Newer ones have been developed that only require a small set of bars with a stand attached not too far from your body.

The first metal bar turnstile detectors identified differences in the electric potential of your body indicating your general mood (tense, relaxed, happy, mad, etc). But the technology has advanced incredibly far. Current high tech ones can determine the levels of hormones in your body, blood composition, sweat response, heart rate, muscle tension levels, and any subtle differences in your mood.

Why are they scanning people this way?

Part of the answer comes from where they use those detectors. They are mainly used where a group of people go into an event that is informational or emotional. Things like school events, sports, amusement parks, and even daily work (coming and going on the subway for example). Each of those events affect people's emotional and intellectual responses, summed up as their mood and ability to be compliant. Changes that take place in a large group of people, from before the event to after the event, can be measured by those turnstile detectors. This information is then used to determine the changes that are needed in those events to make people more compliant.

Outside of watching TV at home, events where you have to pass through turnstile gates are where the largest number of people consistently go for an emotionally satisfying process. Even work, while not satisfying in itself for most people, is how they get money to satisfy their needs. Measuring that level of emotional response is an important part of being able to maintain control over the population at large. There is a reason that those devices are advertised to help with crowd control, although the crowd is much larger and the control is much more subtle than what people are lead to believe.

All this data is analyzed for the benefit of those who really control the events, to see what adjustments are needed to keep the population compliant. The adjustments are varied, some subtle, some not so subtle: building environmental changes like lighting or temperature, rule changes in sports, policy changes at work, uniform changes for colors and patterns, and all sorts of changes you would never notice (are those the same ceiling tiles that were there yesterday, are those the same stadium seats that were here at the last game). A huge amount of continuous testing is ongoing every week at all events people attend.

There is something you can do, however, to throw all their efforts into turmoil. Get yourself emotionally geared up to the opposite of how you feel upon the end of one of those events. They will measure the usually anticipatory emotional responses going into the event. But if you have a set of emotional responses that are outside of expectations coming out of that event, they will have a hard time figuring out how to make adjustments to control you and the population at large.

You will need to change your mood a few minutes before you get to the turnstile metal gate if you want those detectors to measure your new intended mood. It takes that long for all the electro-chemical processes to propagate throughout your body and then be measured by those gates. If you feel happy that your team won, start getting mad or sad before going through the gates. If enough people were to start doing that, those in control would be chasing their tail trying to figure out what to adjust to control everyone.

Chapter 28
Computer Hard Drive Data

When computers first became available to businesses and individuals for home use, the government wanted ways to track what people were doing on those computers. They knew people would try to delete and destroy their data. So the government came up with a plan to copy all of your computer data to hidden location right beside the hard drive.

All information on a computer is held on the hard drive. Older hard drives used a spinning platter technology that wrote data to and read data from metal platters via a magnetic needle device. These platters were encased in a solid metal enclosure. Anyone who took the enclosure apart could see the platters that held their data. (Because of the sensitivity of these parts, opening the enclosure pretty much ensured that the hard drive would no longer work.) While there were programs that could erase all data off the hard drive, there was always a chance that residual magnetic fields on the platters could still hold enough original data to be read by special devices designed to detect those tiny residual magnetic fields. Some people would take the hard drive casing apart and physically destroy the platters that held the data, ensuring the complete destruction of their data. Or so they thought.

That was all a pointless waste of time because a copy of all that data was sitting on the one part of the hard drive that was never destroyed: the hard drive casing.

Long ago government agencies produced a solid hard drive with no spinning platters that could be made into any shape. They built that solid drive into the metal casing of the spinning platter drives that were in use then. All data going into and out of the spinning platters would also be copied to the "hidden" drive in the casing.

This technology for the solid hard drive has since become public and is now used in what are called Solid State Drives, or SSD. New computer SSDs have no spinning platters and no moving parts. They are able to store data in a solid material, and are used the same as regular spinning platter hard drives. But there is still a solid casing covering the SSD.

The process of copying all data from the hard drive to the hidden drive in the casing is still employed on the new SSD drives. They are written to and erased just like the old spinning platter drives. But the casing still retains a copy of every bit ever written to that drive.

So for decades, every bit of data that has ever been recorded has also been saved in the casing. The question is, what has happened to those hard drive casings with all that data?

When you see people advertising that they will pay you to take your non-working computer, some of them are secret government agents taking your computer to get the data off the hard drive casing. And those electronic recycling days where you can drop off your non-working electronics for free, including computers, are just a cover to try to obtain as many hard drives from the public as possible.

When a hard drive stops working, or "crashes", it is actually the hidden drive in the casing getting full. The hidden drive can hold enormous amounts of data, but it does have its limits. When it gets full, it sends a signal to the regular hard drive electronics, which then causes your hard drive to crash. This is the real cause of almost all those crashes.

The crashed drive then gets replaced with a new one, and the old one is thrown out at an electronic recycling center, where is it then promptly handed over to the government agency in charge of collecting all of your data.

Occasionally the government wants access to your data before the hidden drive gets full. To get that access, the government sends out a signal to your computer to crash immediately so that you will have to replace your hard drive and eventually give them complete access to your casing with the hidden drive and all your data on it.

Chapter 29
Elevator Access

Do you ever wonder where those secret government shelters are? The ones they will evacuate government personnel to in case of a large scale attack? Everyone pretty much knows they are underground. But where are the entrances? What special hidden buildings or normal looking houses are sitting over those shelters? The government wants you to be looking for hidden buildings, hidden entrances, and even normal looking houses. But the entrances to those secret shelters are hidden in plain sight. In fact, you have likely been in the doorway of some of them without even realizing it. The entrances are actually normal elevators used by the public in buildings in many cities around the country. And the secret shelters are simply several stories below the buildings with those elevators.

In order to build shelters with no one noticing, they simply put them under new large buildings that would be using elevators. The construction of new buildings is not closely monitored, so extra equipment and material going into the lowest levels is not noticed by the public walking right by the ongoing construction. And the long time it takes to erect some buildings is considered normal.

They use the beginning stages of constructing the lowest levels to start work on secret shelters several stories down. Throughout construction of the building, the shelter is continuously worked on so that excess material is not noticeable during the day to day operations. Some extra material going in one day. Some extra dirt coming out another day. By the time the building is completed, no one will know that a super secret government shelter is several stories below the lowest official level of the building.

To get in to a shelter, you need to take one of the normal elevators used daily by the public in one of those specific buildings. But instead of hitting one of the floor buttons on the elevator, you hold the lowest floor button down while also pushing buttons for the floors 1, 2, 3, and 4 in sequence. Sort of like holding the shift key down on a computer keyboard while typing regular letters to get capital letters. If the lowest floor button on an elevator is the 1st floor, then you hold that button and press 2, 2, 3, 4 in sequence. This floor button code will send the elevator to the shelter several stories below the building you are in.

Regular maintenance is conducted on those shelters. Things like replenishing old food stockpiles, upgrading electronic equipment, changing out batteries, and other normal maintenance. This is conducted by personnel who look like building maintenance people. They bring supplies into the elevator when no one is in it, then press the special button sequence to go to the shelter. The elevator goes back up and into service normally after they get off at the shelter, just like it would for any other floor. When it does however, the elevator floor indicator shows it sitting on a random lower floor until it comes up to a normal level. If you are ever waiting for an elevator and see one stuck on some random lower floor, that is likely because it is going down to the shelter. It takes a couple minutes to go down and back up from that deep underground.

How do they make sure that no unwanted people are using the elevators in case of an emergency so that government people can use them to get to those shelters? Have you noticed that in case of emergencies they tell you to not use elevators? That is how they clear those elevators for use by select personnel. If you don't take elevators during any emergency, you won't be taking them during the specific emergency that will require their use by government personnel to get to their shelter.

114

You can try pressing that sequence of buttons to see if it takes you to an unusually low floor. If it does, the doors will open into a blank looking hallway with a guard standing there. If you do make it to that shelter floor, you may likely never come back. They have holding cells down there specifically for people who are not on the list to be there. But they do not have any spare food for anyone who ends up in those cells. Good luck.

Chapter 30
China's Trojan Horse

China has hit upon a genius idea for attacking the U.S. and has been carrying out that attack for the last few years. Instead of building expensive weapons systems and losing all that money when using them against an enemy (the U.S.), why not have your enemy buy the weapons you want to use against them, and make them pay for delivery to targets in the enemy's own homeland?

How could such a radical idea work? Easily.

First, China has offered ridiculously cheap labor rates to U.S. companies for making products in China, which are then shipped to the U.S. Keep in mind that U.S. companies are paying for all of this.

Second, China has slowly started increasing the use of specific toxic chemicals in those products, chemicals that will slowly debilitate and sicken people who put those items in their homes and businesses; U.S. homes and U.S. businesses. By slowly increasing the use of chemicals, almost no one will notice by the time they reach lethal levels. The unavoidable increase in chemical smell will just be written off as that new product smell.

Third, China is sitting back and raking in money while the U.S. continues to buy more and more of the chemical weapons China is using against them.

In the end, China will have completed a widespread deadly chemical weapons attack against a country that in any other attack situation would have responded with deadly force. In this case however, there will not be one shot fired in response. The U.S. will simply continue to pay for the weapons used to kill themselves.

People have wondered why a strictly communist country like China would offer almost free labor to a capitalist country like the U.S. The standard story is that China is experimenting with the free market. China is actually experimenting, but not with capitalism. They are experimenting with how to add lethal levels of toxic chemicals to consumer products without anyone noticing before it is too late.

Chinese people working in those factories are dying from the levels of toxic chemicals they are working around. But the Chinese government does not care. China has 1.5 billion people. They could lose a few hundred million people and not affect their internal economy nor their national security. They would still have over one billion people left. Because of this huge excess of people, China has no problem sacrificing workers to the goal of eliminating the U.S.

The chemicals China is using are a wide mix. Some of it is just recycled industrial waste to get people in the U.S. accustomed to really odd smells in all those new cheap products from China, and to weaken their immune systems. Some of the chemicals are more specifically designed to stick to a person and work their way into that person's cells in their body, keeping it on a person until it has done all the damage it can. You can identify these chemicals in Chinese products by opening a new item, closing it back up, and seeing if you can smell that weird odor on your clothes and skin. If so, you have just had a chemical weapon attack delivered to you from China via American businesses. These chemicals are currently at a low level as to not make anyone aware of what is happening. If people were to start dropping like flies in the U.S., they would stop buying all those Chinese products before enough Americans were debilitated to make a final takeover by China a stroll in the park.

The types of products that China makes for the U.S. are targeted to have the most effective close contact transmission of those chemicals. They make products used more indoors than outdoors. They make more clothes, toys, appliances, computers, cell phones, indoor furniture, and plastic packaging for food. They make fewer cars or building materials; things used outdoors where the wind dissipates chemicals quickly. They even make air cleaners that add chemicals to the air they are supposed to be cleaning.

While some people in the U.S. are starting to take notice of this attack, China has locked in U.S. companies' profits to the use of cheap Chinese labor. Any attempts to stop this attack will be prevented not by China, but by U.S. companies vigorously defending their right to use cheap Chinese labor, via the usual means of paying off federal and state government officials who will turn a blind eye to anything for enough cash. China even knows how to use America's corrupt political system against itself.

What will future historians write about the U.S. when trying to figure out how it did not see this attack happening. Greek history has the Trojan Horse. Will stories about the end of the U.S. talk about the Chinese Toy?

Epilogue

This book is a collection of paranoid thoughts and ideas. Some might be true, some might not be true. If you think they are all true, then you qualify as being fully paranoid. You can use this as a mirror to find out how paranoid you really are, and how paranoid you should really be.

That being said however, this book does contain information that has been hidden from the public for a long time. How this material came to be compiled in this book will not be disclosed under any circumstances. The people, sources and processes used will not be exposed.

www.ingramcontent.com/pod-product-compliance
Lightning Source LLC
Chambersburg PA
CBHW071156280526
45787CB00002B/516